GREEN GABLES

Lucy Maud Montgomery's Favourite Places

Deirdre Kessler
Photography by Alanna Jankov

Formac Publishing Company Limited
Halifax

Photo credits and other sources, page 71
Design and layout: Andrew Herygers

Formac Publishing Company Limited acknowledges the support of the Cultural Affairs Section, Nova Scotia Department of Tourism and Culture. We acknowledge the financial support of the Government of Canada through the Canada Book Fund for our publishing activities. We acknowledge the support of the Canada Council for the Arts for our publishing program.

Canadian Cataloguing in Publication Data
Kessler, Deirdre
        Green Gables : Lucy Maud Montgomery's
favourite places / Deirdre
Kessler ; photography by Alanna Jankov.

ISBN 978-0-88780-909-5

        1. Montgomery, L. M. (Lucy Maud), 1874-1942—Homes and
haunts—Prince
Edward Island. 2. Literary landmarks—Prince Edward Island.
I. Jankov, Alanna II. Title.

PS8526.O55Z717 2010   813'.52
C2010-900752-2

Formac Publishing Company Limited
5502 Atlantic Street
Halifax, Nova Scotia B3H 1G4
Printed and bound in Canada
www.formac.ca

FILM & CREATIVE INDUSTRIES
NOVA SCOTIA

The Canada Council | Le Conseil des Arts
for the Arts | du Canada

CONTENTS

PREFACE

It was not until after I had been earning my living as a writer and had had five children's novels and five picture books published that I came to learn about the life of L.M. Montgomery and began to visit the sites described in this book — although I had had one encounter with the author's writing three years after adopting Prince Edward Island as my new home. I was a teacher at Vernon River Consolidated School and had read many of my own favourite children's books to my Grade 3 class — *Charlotte's Web, Heidi, Tom Sawyer* — when I decided to see what the fuss over Montgomery was about. I pulled a dog-eared copy of *Anne of Green Gables* from the shelves of the school library and began to read it aloud to the children. I did not read the novel beforehand, which was my usual practice, and so when we arrived at the penultimate chapter, "The Reaper Whose Name Is Death," I was not prepared for Matthew Cuthbert's death. My throat thickened. Tears filled my eyes. I stopped reading and sat silently on the chair by the window, where we always gathered for storytime. At my feet on the floor and in little chairs in a tight semi-circle were all of the children I had come to love over the past two years. I closed the book, and we all sat completely still, trying to find a place for the sorrow that had entered our lives when Matthew collapsed in the porch doorway. And then, one child said, "I didn't know a teacher could cry."

Many years later, from 1997 to 2000, when I was co-chair of the L.M. Montgomery Institute at the University of Prince Edward Island, I had the privilege of getting to know members of Montgomery's family and of meeting and working with Montgomery scholars, researchers, site interpreters and fans from around the world. The people associated with Montgomery have in common a deep respect and affection for a writer who is able to make a direct link between the emotional lives of her characters and the interior lives of her readers, a writer whose profound connection with the land and sea of her Island home inspires readers to look anew at the natural world around them.

Deirdre Kessler
Charlottetown, P.E.I.

INTRODUCTION

Lucy Maud Montgomery changed Prince Edward Island. There exists an overlay of her vision of the place on top of the physical island. Since 1908, in dozens of countries worldwide, millions of readers of Montgomery's novels have imagined Prince Edward Island in their minds' eyes and thus have added strength to Montgomery's vision and contributed to a liminal dimension of the geographical place, a dimension that is sensed by residents and visitors alike. The literary landscape and the actual landscape have melded so that it is difficult to separate Montgomery's Island and her influence from the source of her inspiration.

The pilgrimages that millions of readers of *Anne of Green Gables* have made to the fictional setting of the novel and to the author's birthplace, to her Cavendish home and to her cousins' Park Corner home are testament to the endurance of Montgomery's art and her ability to connect with the human heart, no matter what the reader's age, era, gender or country of origin.

This book presents a tour of these four favourite sites, highlighting the landmarks and the artifacts that relate Montgomery's life and times to the present day. Each site is tended carefully by Islanders. The Green Gables house is furnished in accordance with descriptions from *Anne of Green Gables* and has been owned and run by Parks Canada for many years.

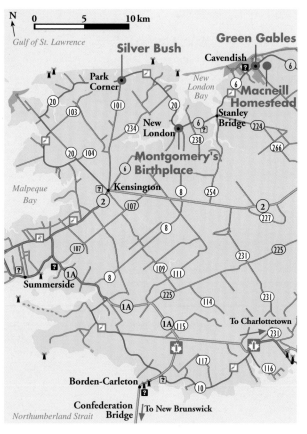

The Cavendish home where Montgomery lived with her Macneill grandparents no longer is standing; however, the property is owned and lovingly cared for by descendants, John and Jennie Macneill, and is open to the public. The Birthplace at New London (Clifton Corner) was donated to the Province of Prince Edward Island and is operated by the Lucy Maud Montgomery Foundation. The house is a museum of Montgomery memorabilia and furnished in late nineteenth-century style. The Campbells at Park Corner have also generously opened their family home as a museum to the memory of Lucy Maud Montgomery.

Following the chapters on these four sites and a look at farming and rural life of one hundred years ago, there is a biography of the author and an account of her life as a writer.

Whether you visit Montgomery's favourite places in person or through the photographs and text of this book, we are sure you will appreciate the contribution one woman has made both to a small island in the Gulf of St. Lawrence and to the wide world beyond its shores. Maud Montgomery deeply cherished her home and articulated this profound love of place for all of us, so that we might see and feel and think as she did, and perhaps, return in our own way something of her affection for Prince Edward Island.

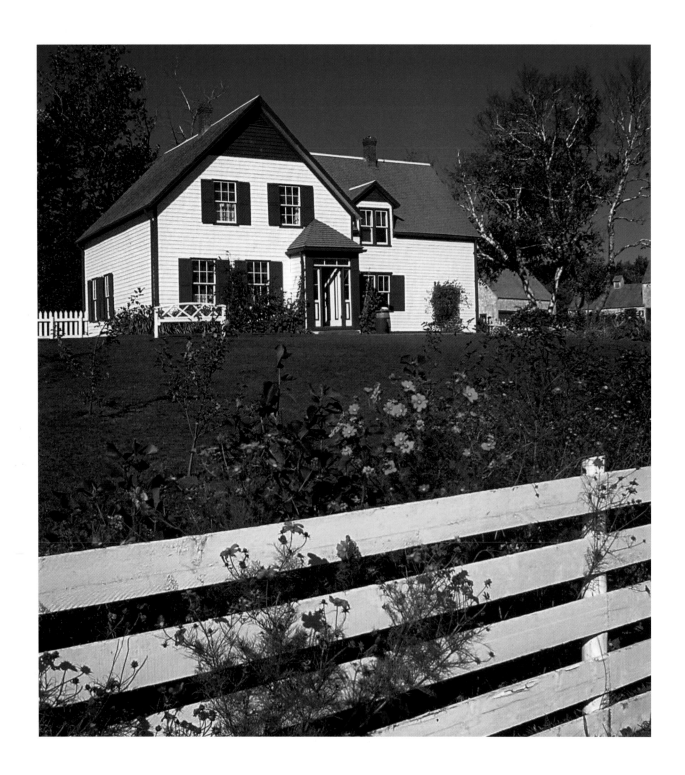

GREEN GABLES

In hopes of matching reality with their mental images of the Island home of Canada's favourite orphan, Anne Shirley, several hundred thousand people visit the Green Gables site in Prince Edward Island National Park each year. In 1908, when Montgomery's first novel was published, Samuel Clemens wrote to the author to say that with Anne she had written "the sweetest creation of child life since the immortal Alice." High praise, indeed, from the writer who, under his *nom de plume*, Mark Twain, created the equally immortal Tom Sawyer and Huck Finn.

What visitors seek and find at Green Gables is a smooth blend of reality and fiction; in fact, the melding of the two elements is so seamless that many people still regard Anne as a real person, even after a thorough explanation of how the Green Gables house in Cavendish really belonged to Montgomery's relatives, David Jr. and Margaret Macneill,

cousins of the author's grandfather, and served only as a model for the home of the fictional sister and brother, Marilla and Matthew Cuthbert, of make-believe Avonlea. In the end, the long-standing confusion between fact and fantasy is high tribute to the author, although she herself was often annoyed by readers who constantly asked her whether such-and-such was the original in her books. "Green Gables was drawn from David Macneill's house, now Mr. Webb's — though not so much the house itself as the situation and scenery," Montgomery wrote in her journal on Friday, January 27, 1911. "And the truth of my description of it is attested by the fact that everybody has recognized it." In this same journal entry, Montgomery admits to having her own sense of Anne's reality: "For she is and always has been, from the moment I first thought of her, so real to me that I feel I am doing violence to something when I deny her an existence anywhere save in Dreamland. Does she not stand at my elbow even now — if I turned my head quickly should I not see her ...?"

Opposite: *Green Gables House*
Top: *'Anne' on the bridge*

VISITOR CENTRE

The visitor centre at the Parks Canada Green Gables site provides a multimedia overview of the property and the experience. Perhaps what first draws the eye is the small Royal typewriter that Montgomery purchased nearly new in 1906 on which the typescript for Anne of Green Gables was prepared. While she was alive, Montgomery gave the typewriter to a friend, Edwin Smith; later, Smith's widow gave it to the government of Prince Edward Island before the Green Gables house became part of the National Park.

Parks Canada has a display of first or early editions of Montgomery's novels and correspondence between the author and some of her fans. For example, there is a letter to Richard Scott (Jack) Lewis of Virginia written by Montgomery in 1927 from her Norval, Ontario, home. Also on display are two signed sheets in the author's own hand of her "Island Hymn," which she composed in 1908. "Fair Island of the sea/We raise our song to thee/The bright and blest," begins the first of the three-stanza hymn Montgomery wrote a few months before *Anne of Green Gables* was published. At the time, Montgomery was the organist and Sunday school teacher at the Cavendish Presbyterian Church. Harry Watts, a professor of the Charlottetown School of Music, decided the Island needed its own hymn, so he wrote to Montgomery in Cavendish to ask her to compose lyrics, to the melody of

Top Left: *Lobby of the Visitor Centre*
Top Right: *Letters written by Montgomery*
Above: *Montgomery's typewriter*

"God Save the King," which might be suitable for singing at dignified state occasions. Montgomery composed the lyrics, and Watts then had Lawrence W. Watson, the organist at St. Peter's Anglican Cathedral in Charlottetown, compose the music. A copy of Watson's handwritten score sits beside Montgomery's lyrics at the Green Gables visitors' centre. All these documents and artifacts are housed in a climate-controlled case heavily insulated with silica gel, with a fan to control dust. Open for curious hands to touch, however, is a replica of some pages from one of Montgomery's scrapbooks complete with a patch of fur from one of her beloved cats, sprigs of flora, colourful montages of flowers made from magazine pictures and articles clipped from local newspapers. One wall of the visitors' centre boasts a diorama of artist Ben Stahl's portrayal of Anne against a multilayered Island landscape. And, playing in rotation in two small theatres at the visitors' centre is a seven-minute film titled *What a Small Big World It Is*, created by the Armadillo Company.

PERSON OF NATIONAL HISTORIC SIGNIFICANCE

When guests leave the visitors' centre through doors that open out onto a compound visually protected from the large parking lot by the angular visitors' centre, there is much to behold: plantings of wild rose bushes, red osier dogwoods and other native Island flora. There is also a red sandstone monument; a tribute to Montgomery. The monument is a stone cairn, one metre high with a bronze plaque in French and English that reads "to the enduring fame of Lucy Maud Montgomery." The Historic Sites and Monuments Board of Canada erected the monument in 1943, a year after the author's death.

In 1937, the Canadian government designated 40 kilometres of north shore land as the Prince Edward Island National Park, including Green Gables, the cultural landmark. From the time *Anne of Green Gables* was published early in the twentieth century, people would seek out Green Gables, knocking on the door of the farmhouse then owned by Myrtle and Ernest Webb. Myrtle Macneill Webb was a niece of David and Margaret Macneill, the original homeowners. Before long, the site became a shrine to Montgomery readers around the world. Today, several walking trails, open year round, radiate from

Replica of a page from one of Montgomery's scrapbooks

Manuscript for music of "Island Hymn." Montgomery wrote the words.

Green Gables, including the Haunted Wood and Balsam Hollow trails. Even in winter Green Gables hosts a plethora of activities, when visitors can make an appointment to see the house or they may use the Green Gables ski trail anytime. No matter which season visitors choose, they will find the landscape immortalized in Montgomery's most famous work:

> Below the garden a green field lush with clover sloped down to the hollow where the brook ran and where scores of white birches grew, upspringing airily out of an undergrowth suggestive of delightful possibilities in ferns and mosses and woodsy things generally. Beyond it was a hill, where the gray gable end of the little house she had seen from the other side of the Lake of Shining Waters was visible.
>
> Off to the left were the big barns and beyond them, away down over the green, low-sloping fields, was the sparkling blue glimpse of sea.
>
> Anne's beauty-loving eyes lingered on it all, taking everything greedily in; she had looked on so many unlovely places in her life, poor child; but this was as lovely as anything she had ever dreamed.

BARN, FARMYARD AND GARDEN

The Green Gables farm, which now has reconstructed barns and outbuildings of a traditional Island farmyard and the late nineteenth-century-styled gardens, was first settled in 1831 by David Macneill Sr., who was an uncle of Montgomery's grandfather, Alexander Macneill. An enlarged, laminated copy of a page from the 1880 edition of *Meacham's Illustrated Historical Atlas of Prince Edward Island* can be seen in the barn. The page shows the lay of the land around Cavendish as well as the division into mostly long, narrow, 100-acre plots of land, including the farm belonging to David Macneill Sr. On this map, it is evident that the brook that burbles through Green Gables originates about a mile to the south-southeast on what was Alexander Laird's property, across the Mayfield Road (now Route 13) and through five properties south of the Cavendish graveyard corner.

(Back, left to right) Margaret Macneill, David Macneill, Myrtle Webb; (front) Marion Webb on Ernest Webb's knee (1907)

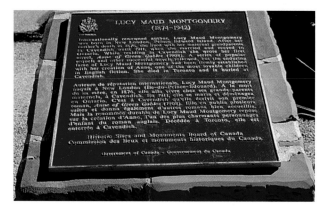

Above: *Monument to L.M. Montgomery outside the Visitor Centre*
Opposite: *Garden at Green Gables*

The brook flows through the Haunted Wood and into the pond at the main gate of Green Gables. The pond then flows into the Gulf of St. Lawrence. "The brook that runs below the Cuthbert place and through Lynde's Hollow is, of course, my own dear brook of the woods which runs below Webb's and through 'Pierce's Hollow,'" Montgomery wrote in her journal. Maud — as she was commonly called — Montgomery and her Macneill cousins would have walked along the banks of the brook and the pond all the way to the gulf, and they would have been familiar with every twist and turn. In her youthful autobiography, *The Alpine Path* (1917), Montgomery writes about the "fun in abundance, simple, wholesome, delightful fun, with our playhouses and

Top: *Barn and outbuildings*
Above: *Map of lots around Cavendish, 1880*

our games in the beautiful summer twilights, when we ranged happily through fields and orchards."

Today, the barn at Green Gables is based on photographs of the original Webb barn. It measures about 24 by 7 metres, with a high, steeply pitched hip roof and two lofts; the smaller one for straw, the larger for hay. An old hay-fork hangs from the ridge-pole over the central floor of the barn. Off to one side of the main barn floor is a blue-painted threshing machine made by Thomas Hall Manufacturing Company in Summerside, "P.E. Island." A "Farm Life" exhibit is located in a room at the northwest corner of the barn's main level. Horses' harnesses, barrels, potato sacks and a turnip seeder are also kept here — all of the paraphernalia of a working farm.

In the lower level of the barn, where horses and cows traditionally would have been kept, there is a specially built theatre that shows a Parks Canada film about the life of L.M. Montgomery called *A Celebration of the Imagination*. Written by Deirdre Kessler and produced by Michael Willoughby of Bristol Group's Ad Vantage Productions, this 16-minute video shares a synopsis of the Montgomery's life and a sense of the literary legacy she imparted to Canada and to the rest of the world. A replica of a life-sized cow standing in the west wing of the upper barn is a favourite of city children, who might never before have had such a close encounter with a cow — real or statuary.

The farmyard to the south of the barn includes a granary and woodshed. In the west end of the barn is a canteen where homemade cookies and other food reminiscent of nineteenth-century refreshments are sold, including locally made raspberry cordial. The gardens have been designed to represent typical Island farm gardens, with sweetpeas, phlox, sunflowers, lettuce, corn, wax beans, beets, parsnips, carrots, potatoes and other vegetables and flowers. Century-old lilac and snowball trees and old rose bushes surround the house, decorative shrubs that might have been brought from Scotland by ship, carefully wrapped and protected until they were planted in the earth at the new homestead.

Top: *View of the farm and barn from the golf course (1938)*
Middle: *Anita Webb in front of the barn (1920)*
Bottom: *Threshing machine*

A HOUSE FACING EAST

Green Gables faces the rising sun and is nestled midway up a hill overlooking a brook. Beyond the brook stands a grove of tall spruce and mixed hardwoods. The original house was built in 1831, and is today the kitchen wing. The front entrance of the house has a wide, thick, Island-stone front step, with marks from the stonecarver's chisel still evident. In the 1870s, the house was enlarged and a storey-and-a-half wing with a parlour, dining/sitting room and five small bedrooms was added. At the end of the First World War, the kitchen roof was raised and three additional bedrooms and storage rooms were added. This

Top Left: *Making butter*
Top Right: *Main entrance to Green Gables House*
Opposite: *Beans, corn and marigolds in the garden at Green Gables*

is the shape and size of the house today. Parks Canada undertook a major restoration of Green Gables in 1985 to create a house museum furnished according Montgomery's descriptions in the Anne books, in a period circa 1880.

Above: *Two views of Green Gables House, today (top), and in the 1920s (below)*
Opposite: *Furnishings in the parlour*

PARLOUR

To the immediate left of the front entrance is the parlour Anne called "a dark and gloomy apartment," with late-nineteenth-century-style furnishings: a horsehair settee, armchair and rocker, the arms and backs of which are protected with antimacassars. There is also a small Mason and Hamlin pump organ, an ornate cast-iron grate covering the fireplace opening and a lambrequin, or mantle cloth, formally draped on the mantlepiece. The hand-hooked, floral-patterned mat and shadow boxes with fabric flower and human-hair wreathes are all examples of Victorian fancy-work. Two heavily draped east-facing windows look toward the Haunted Wood. A second door in the parlour leads to the dining/sitting room.

DINING/SITTING ROOM

The dining/sitting room has two large south-facing windows looking out upon the fenced yard with its old lilac and snowball trees; beyond them are the farm's fields, which are now fairways of the Green Gables golf course. The beginning of Lover's Lane can also be seen from here, as can the east slope leading to the brook, which is sometimes called the Balsam Hollow Brook. On a corner table is a concertina; a gilt-titled volume, *The Ladies Wreath*; a stereoscopic viewer; and a potted fern. China in the dining-room cabinet includes some of the delicate rosebud-spray pattern that readers of *Anne of Green Gables* know was Marilla's good set of china. On the dining-room table sits more of the rosebud china, sparklingly clean as if

Top left: *Dining table*
Bottom left: *Sitting area*
Top right: *Fireplace and mantelpiece in the parlour*
Above: *Dining room wallpaper detail*

ready for an afternoon visit from the minister or a church committee meeting. The wallpaper pattern in the dining room is a geometric, green ivy design, which adds to the formality of the room. The kitchen can be seen through a second door in the dining room; here the house takes on a less formal ambiance.

MATTHEW'S ROOM

In keeping with the character's humility, the unadorned bedroom known as Matthew's room is large enough only for essentials: a high, single bed covered with a homespun woolen blanket, a washstand, a pine trunk and a chair. Matthew's bowler hat sits on the chair, as do his good woolen vest and trousers, which he would have saved to wear on Sundays and to attend funerals and Anne's school concerts. On the floor lies a hooked mat in a maple-leaf-and-log design that seems to suit the old bachelor whom Anne, and nearly all readers of Montgomery's first novel, came to love fiercely. A single window looks from Matthew's room out to the barnyard. His room is a few steps away from the kitchen's woodstove, which he would

Above: *Furninshings and details in Matthew's Room*

have had to have stoked throughout cold winter nights. A downstairs bedroom traditionally would have been used for the infirm or for nursing mothers, but as we learn from Montgomery's first Anne novel, Matthew's heart was weak and he could not take the stress of going up and down the stairs.

KITCHEN

The wainscotted kitchen at Green Gables is more than three metres wide and eight meters long. Everything in the room has a place and a purpose. This part of the original building has the ambiance of nearly two hundred years of care, right down to the foot-worn wooden floors. At the north end by the back porch is the laundry corner, where a wooden ironing board topped with a smaller sleeve ironing board and heavy irons stands ready for use. Nearby is a glass Crystal Globe scrub-board, a galvanized-wire hand agitator in a large wash basin, and a wooden rack for drying clothing indoors during inclement weather.

Near the laundry corner against the east wall is a drop-leaf pine table with a tablecloth, and a loaf of fresh bread. Across from it is a large New Waterloo No. 2 cast-iron woodstove with its three tiers for cooking and oval

Kitchen and Furnishings

peekaboo oven with an ornate door embossed with the words: "Fire King Oven Patented C. Fawcett, Sackville, N.B." Under the east-facing double kitchen windows is a leather couch, and further along the same wall is a ceiling-high pine cupboard with four open shelves, three drawers and two lower compartments. Contemporary kitchen designers have found new value for such commodious storage space.

PANTRY AND DAIRY PORCH

There are three preparation and storage rooms attached to the long kitchen: a back porch, where visitors exit from the house tour, a pantry; and a dairy porch. The pantry contains a second ceiling-high, two-metre-wide pine cupboard filled to the brim with utensils and tureens, a pedestal cake plate, everyday china, platters and crocks. Here is the "old brown-and-white set" of dishes that Marilla used for everyday, as opposed to the rosebud-spray set that was saved for company and special occasions. There is a pastry table for rolling dough and kneading bread, and a high shelf opposite the pine cupboard holds an array of cooking aids and home remedies in tins and cork-topped bottles and crocks. These include a large bottle of vanilla extract, liquid stains in crock bottles, stove blacking and stovepipe varnish. A label on a cork-topped bottle reads "Johnson's Emulsion of Pure Cod Liver Oil with Hypophosphites of Lime & Soda for all Pulmonary Affections, Emaciation and general debility," which was procured from Johnson & Johnson Druggists of Charlottetown and Souris, Prince Edward Island (the label was printed by Haszard & Moore Printers). Anodyne liniment — the same medicinal substance that Anne Shirley mistakenly puts into the cake she made for the minister — rests in a blue-green embossed bottle. (Montgomery said she got the idea for that particular incident from something that happened while she was teaching school in Bideford and boarding at the nearby Methodist parsonage. There, the mistress of the parsonage accidentally flavoured a layer cake with anodyne liniment and fed a piece to a visiting minister.) On the floor in the pantry is a round, wooden,

Pantry shelves

five-headed spring mousetrap and a basket of yarn, which readers can identify from the Anne novels as the basket into which Anne strained milk by mistake.

The dairy-porch, which has one low window, provides access to the well-house and barnyard through a south-facing door. The well-house outside the dairy-porch door was reconstructed from an 1895 photograph of the Webb house. In the photograph, Myrtle Macneill Webb is sitting outside the house. In fact, the reconstruction of the pantry, kitchen, and parlour were inspired by Montgomery's own photographs, especially those of the Campbell kitchen. In the porch floor is the hatch that covers the steps leading down to the cellar, where root vegetables and jars and crocks of preserves would be stored. Milk would be brought from the barn back to the dairy porch to be strained and then left to settle, so that the cream could rise to the top; later, the cream would be skimmed off

: *Pantry shelves*

and saved for making into butter and cheese. Attached to a food-preparation table is a food mill or meat grinder.

ANNE'S EAST GABLE BEDROOM

By walking up the twelve steps of the front staircase, visitors will arrive at Anne's room, which is cordoned off in the east gable of the house. The room looks out over the brook, Haunted Wood and Orchard Slope. In the distance, a row of tall spruce trees lines the ridge that parallels Route 13, the main road from the south leading from Hunter River to Cavendish. Anne's bed is made of iron and brass; the iron is painted white and the brass is polished. There is a patterned, white coverlet of cotton and linen on the bed. A feather tick rests atop metal

Top: *Photograph taken in 1895 showing Myrtle Macneill Webb sitting by the tree, and showing the small well house*
Above: *View from Anne's bedroom window*

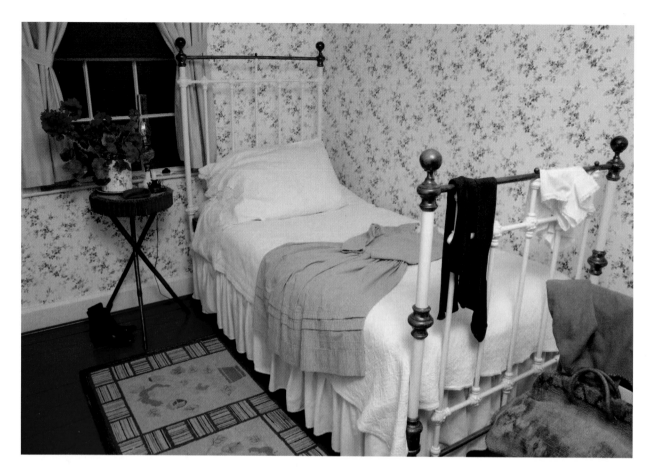

Anne's bedroom with one of her everday dresses.

springs; the high mound of feathers makes the bed look inviting to anyone who likes to flop on puffy bedclothes, and is especially tempting to children who like to jump on springy beds. Two examples of workaday clothes Anne might have worn are arranged neatly on the coverlet — a brown, patched and plain orphanage dress and a slightly fancier homespun seersucker dress. But the garment that attracts the most attention is the brown gloria puff-sleeved creation hanging in the open closet door. With its lace-detailed high neck and silky fabric, this is the dress that made Anne exclaim, "Oh, it seems to me this must be a happy dream."

Anne took the dress and looked at it in reverent silence. Oh, how pretty it was — a lovely soft brown gloria with all the gloss of silk; a skirt with dainty frills and shirrings; a waist elaborately pintucked in the most fashionable way, with a little ruffle of filmy lace at the neck. But the sleeves — they were the crowning glory! Long elbow cuffs, and above them two beautiful puffs divided by rows of shirring and bows of brown silk ribbon.

"That's a Christmas present for you, Anne," said Matthew shyly. "Why — why — Anne, don't you like it? Well now — well now."

For Anne's eyes had suddenly filled with tears.

The small bookshelves on the wall by the closet hold a robin's nest, a blue pitcher and a photograph that readers will notice is similar to the one of herself Miss Stacy gave to Anne. The old carpet-bag that Anne was carrying when she arrived at Green Gables sits on a chair. On the bedside table, which is covered with a fringed hooked mat, is a mirror, a pin cushion, a candle and a book. On the window ledge are a few blue mussel and clam shells, and the earth-red painted pine floors are covered with faded hooked mats — one of flowerpots filled with flowers. A flow-blue chamber set on a commode and a broken school slate on a small wooden chest complete the remaining furnishings.

Over the years, Green Gables curators have interpreted Montgomery's description of Anne's room in various ways. Photographs and postcards from the 1950s, 1960s and 1970s depict different furnishings and decor reflective of the various curatorial visions. The current decor is true to the 1880s, the period in which the first of Montgomery's Anne books is set.

Top left: *Dress of "soft brown gloria"*
Top right: *Books and bird's nest in Anne's room*

MARILLA'S ROOM

Over the door leading into Marilla Cuthbert's room, a transom light provides additional natural light to the otherwise dark upstairs hallway. One of the oldest artifacts at Green Gables covers the floor in this room: a large, handwoven rug of wool warp and cotton weft with a pattern of woodland flowers and ferns in yellow ochre on a red-and-white background. The overshot coverlet on the bed is also red and white. On the bedside table is an amethyst brooch much like the one described in the novel that caused Anne so much trouble. One west window allows light to enter the room assigned to stern, pious Marilla Cuthbert. All of the artifacts reflect the author's tone for Marilla's character: a Bible and spectacles on the bedside table, a photograph of a woman one assumes is Marilla and Matthew's mother, a black lace shawl and hat pins, and, on the wall, a sepia print of a town with

Furnishings from Marilla's Room

*Objects and clothing
from Marilla's Room*

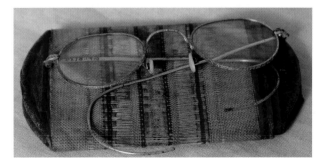

Sewing machine

seven churches. On the commode is a complete chamber set of flow-blue china, which one could imagine was a prized possession of Marilla's Scottish immigrant parents.

SEWING ROOM
Before Green Gables became part of the National Park, Louise Lowther, the daughter of Keith Webb and granddaughter of Myrtle and Ernest Webb, slept in what is now the sewing room. It is the largest room in the old portion of the upstairs, and it has a lovely view west toward the barnyard. The sewing machine is in front of the window, so the seamstress could clearly see anyone coming and going from the house. The back door would have been used for all but special company. An umbrella swift for winding wool, now quite fragile, stands on a drop-leaf table along with carding hands and a cheese box for storing wool. A hit-and-miss-patterned hooked rug made by Irene Seaman Ramsay circa 1930 is spread on the floor, and all of the items required to mend the family's clothing are kept neatly in Mi'kmaq and Chinese baskets. Adjacent to the sewing room is a narrow storage area that was created when the second floor of the kitchen ell was expanded. There's a little low window looking out onto Lover's Lane from the west end of the storage space; the dimensions and cosiness of this corner are inviting to those who like to read on a rainy afternoon in such a snug window nook.

LOVER'S LANE
"I would exchange all the kingdoms of the world for a sunset ramble in Lover's Lane," Montgomery wrote to her

 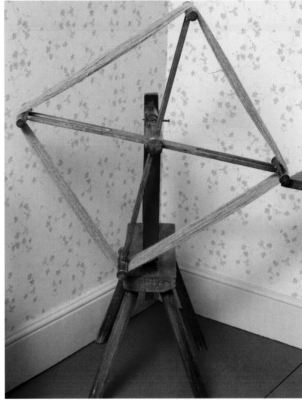

Left: *Spinning wheel*   **Right:** *Wool winder*

friend George MacMillan. The lane made famous in the Anne series has a real incarnation a short distance from the Green Gables house. Here the lane becomes Balsam Hollow trail, which upholds Montgomery's love of nature as its theme. "I had always a deep love of nature," the author wrote in *The Alpine Path*. "A little fern growing in the woods, a shallow sheet of June-bells under the firs, moonlight falling on the ivory column of a tall birch, an evening star over the old tamarack on the dyke, shadow-waves rolling over a field of ripe wheat — all gave me 'thoughts that lay too deep for tears' and feelings which I had then no vocabulary to express." When Montgomery was writing her first Anne novels, there would have been no Green Gables golf course as there is now, but only the farm fields with their "shadow-waves" of grain and the quiet of seasons in the woodland. It is perhaps on walks

through Lover's Lane, Haunted Wood and other places Montgomery revered that one can come to understand the depth of inspiration the author received from her surroundings. Many are surprised to discover that Montgomery spent nearly half of her life in Ontario, far away from Cavendish, and yet nineteen of her twenty novels are set in Prince Edward Island; never did she lose her passion for the woods, shores and farmlands of her youth.

HAUNTED WOOD
The Haunted Wood trail begins below the house, where the hill slopes to the alder-lined creek and songbirds nest in the thick undergrowth. Balsam firs, white and yellow birch, maples and old poplars covered with yellow lichen

grow on the slope that rises from the creek to a ridge parallel to the Mayfield Road, currently called Route 13. In season, red-winged blackbirds, white-throated sparrows, chickadees and yellow warblers sing their hearts out in the Haunted Wood and its adjacent fields. These are just a few of the more than 300 species of birds that nest on the Island. Occasionally a blue heron will startle a visitor when it emerges from the pond and flies away toward the gulf. It is not unusual to see foxes in the Haunted Wood, and red squirrels will alert the woods to your presence with their high, insistent chatter. The resonant caw of crows, the loud, repetitious flick or flicker of the aptly named yellow-shafted flicker and its shrill descending "*kee-oo*" are common here. Underfoot in May are sweet mayflowers or trailing arbutus; in June the summer series of blooming flowers begins, which can make an unsuspecting visitor swoon at the sight of so many lupins,

Top: *Brook on the Balsam Hollow trail*
Above: *'Anne' on the Haunted Wood trail*

Balsam Hollow trail

Above: *Site of L.M. Montgomery's Cavendish home*

daisies, purple vetch, red and orange hawkweed — Montgomery did not conjure up the Island flora she described so passionately. Each season brings its own delights; from early spring through the depths of winter the woodlands are alive with sound, sight and scent. In summer, wild strawberries, raspberries and blueberries grow in fields and hedgerows. All around Green Gables, the nearby shore in the National Park and the rest of Cavendish, you can recognize elements from Montgomery's Anne novels. "Cavendish is to a large extent Avonlea," Montgomery wrote in her journal on Friday, January 27, 1911. Montgomery based Green Gables on the farmhouse and especially on the property belonging to David Jr. and Margaret MacNeill, her cousins.

If you made a bee-line east from Green Gables down the slope to the brook, across the bridge, up through the Haunted Wood, along the south side of the cemetery and across the Mayfield Road, you would arrive at the lane leading to the Macneill homestead. If you walked quickly, the journey might take you seven minutes. The dyked, bowered lane to the Macneill homestead was well-trod by Montgomery, who travelled frequently between her Grandmother and Grandfather Macneill's place and the house that is now called Green Gables. From the graveyard hill, Montgomery said she could see the blue gulf waters, and it was there that she chose to be buried. The fields between the cemetery and the north shore are now thick with spruce, but the sound of the surf pounding on the shore can still be heard from the hill that lies halfway between the beloved home of Montgomery's Macneill grandparents and the Green Gables farm and woodlands where she spent so many happy hours.

L.M. MONTGOMERY'S CAVENDISH HOME

Living history, indeed: the current owners of the Macneill homestead in Cavendish are John and Jennie Macneill, who live in a farmhouse adjacent to the homestead property and operate the site. John is the great-grandson of Alexander and Lucy Macneill, the maternal grandparents of L.M. Montgomery. The farmland has passed down through generations of Macneills, who were among the early Scots settlers of Prince Edward Island. John and Jennie Macneill developed the homestead site after the publication of the first volume of L.M. Montgomery's journals. It was then that they knew exactly how the author felt about her home: "It is and ever must be hallowed ground to me," Montgomery wrote. The word "hallowed" may sound overly dramatic, but even the most casual visitor to the site of L.M. Montgomery's Cavendish home must acknowledge its powerful spirit. Jennie Macneill writes that before she and John began its restoration, the area "was a jungle of fallen trees, stumps, thorn bushes and debris. It took us two years to clean out the cellar of the farmhouse, put back the stones that had fallen in, dig out the well and the old homestead lane,

Top: The Macneills' house, showing L.M. Montgomery's bedroom window on the upper storey

clean up the wooded area, plant gardens and flowers, and set it all up back to rights."

Although the old house is now gone, its foundation and deep sandstone cellar project a numinous presence. Wide stepstones that once graced the kitchen lead to the cellar. Marks from the stonecutter's chisel are clearly seen on most of the large, red, Island foundation stones. Almost in the centre of the cellar is a massive sandstone base that once supported the fireplaces and joists. It is easy to imagine how secure and cosy the Macneill family home was, protected by a grove of spruce trees to the north. The spruces buffered the sometimes fierce Gulf of St. Lawrence winds. To the west, and partly along the south face, are more trees — balm of Gilead or poplars, apple trees and birches.

L.M. Montgomery lived with her grandparents in the Macneill home from the time she was twenty-one months old until she was thirty-six. It was in Grandmother and Grandfather Macneill's house that Montgomery wrote *Anne of Green Gables* — the novel for which she is most famous. Montgomery loved walking the bowered homestead lane to the west of the house, which took her to the cemetery where her mother and grandparents are now buried, to the dell beyond it, and to the farm belonging

Montgomery's photograph of the kitchen in her grandparents' home (1890s)

Above: *Trail through the woods*
Inset: *New Cavendish post office*

to her cousins, David and Margaret Macneill, and the house that is now called Green Gables. As Montgomery walked up the lane, returning from a visit, she would "see the kitchen light shining through the trees." Today you can tread the same path up the lane to the same bend in the lane, and although the farmhouse and outbuildings are gone, the poplars and one original apple tree standing sentinel around the deep sandstone cellar of the Macneill home remain. "The peace and quiet of this dear old spot is very sweet to me," Montgomery wrote. "There is no place on earth I love, or ever will love as I do it."

A fenced path leading north from the homestead serves as the shortcut to the church; the route took Montgomery through a grove of spruces and along the edge of a meadow, which still blooms with some of the myriad of wildflowers the author loved so much: ox-eyed daisies, purple vetch, hawkweed and wild roses. The woodsy fragrances of fern and sun-warmed hay still permeate the air in late summer. The Cavendish church, where Montgomery's secret fiancé, Ewan Macdonald, was minister for three years, faces the gulf-shore highway and the Gulf of St. Lawrence. In 1973, a traditional Island farmhouse with architecture similar to the original Macneill house

was moved to the property beside the Cavendish church and was turned into a post office.

As the crow flies, it is a short distance to the north from the Macneill homestead to the Cavendish shore, and on windy days, even in the protection of the homestead site, waves can be heard crashing on the shore. The hillfields to the south and east of the Macneill homestead have changed little since the days when Montgomery explored them. She loved the "woodsy nooks" and the "oddity of fence and shape," which turned the fields into characters for her. John and Jennie Macneill annually plant gardens much like those the author would have planted. Montgomery delighted in gardens and gardening: "It is the greatest pleasure my days bring me to go out to my garden every morning and see what new blossoms have opened over night."

A touchstone for Montgomery long after she moved away from Prince Edward Island was the peace and quiet of the Macneill homestead. She pays tribute to the place many times, both directly in her journals and letters and indirectly in her fiction. She understood "how deeply rooted and strong" was her love for the homestead; indeed,

Stamps and desk from when Maud Montgomery and her grandparents ran the post office

she attributed the development of her literary gift to the years she lived in Cavendish.

The Cavendish post office was, for many years, in the kitchen of the Macneill home. As Jennie Macneill writes, "Alexander was the Cavendish postmaster from 1870 to 1898. When he died, his wife took over, with Maud as her assistant. The post office was kept in the farmhouse kitchen, which was a great help to Maud. She mailed her manuscripts to various publishers. No one knew of her rejections or acceptances because the post office was right in her own house, and corresponding with publishers was Maud's own secret. In a small community where everyone knew every else's business, this was very important to Maud." In May of 1905 Montgomery began to write *Anne of Green Gables*, completing the story in January of 1906 and then typing it on "an old second-hand typewriter that never makes the capitals plain and won't print 'w' at all." From the kitchen post office she sent the manuscript first to Bobbs-Merrill in Indianapolis, who promptly rejected

it. She then mailed the story to MacMillan Company in New York City, who also rejected it. Next, she sent it to Lothrop, Lee and Shepard in Boston, and then to the Henry Holt Company of New York. The manuscript was rejected each time, which always discouraged her, but she was not humiliated by having all of Cavendish know about her lack of success because only she saw the package come and go. Montgomery put the manuscript away in a hat box for a year before trying to find another publisher for it. In the summer of 1907 she sent it to the L.C. Page Company in Boston, and this time she was successful.

The original Cavendish post office scales, seal and desk are now housed in a bookstore at the edge of the Macneill homestead site along with other artifacts from the author's life, including a porthole and a telescope salvaged from the *Marco Polo*, a schooner that was wrecked on the Cavendish shore on July 25, 1883, when Montgomery was nine. The event fired her imagination, and her poem, "The Wreck of the *Marco Polo*," was one of her earliest published pieces.

Red squirrels chatter warnings to one another when you approach the Macneill homestead. Kinglets and chickadees tweet and chitter as they flit in the birch and choke-cherry trees, and you'll likely see a family of robins by the edge of the garden waiting for John Macneill to hoe around the root vegetables and unearth worms for them. And when Jennie Macneill gives you a tour of the site, she doesn't need to read the quotations excerpted from Montgomery's works on plaques discreetly placed around the property; Jennie knows the author's words by heart. Long before she married into the Macneill family, young Jennie Moore was a fan of L.M. Montgomery, reading the author's books in the one-room Cavendish school she at-tended, the same school where Montgomery herself had been a student. Jennie clearly remembers Montgomery's state funeral held one day in late April of 1942. On that day, Jennie squeezed into a pew to watch and listen as her childhood heroine was eulogized. Jennie Macneill never forgets the power, dignity, passion and intelligence Montgomery brought not only to her literary works, but also to every task that faced her.

THE BIRTHPLACE AT CLIFTON CORNER

"A dream fulfilled in coming here — very emotional!" So wrote one of the thousands of yearly visitors to the Lucy Maud Montgomery birthplace. Others wrote "awesome" and "very authentic."

The curator of the birthplace site says that it is not unusual for people from five or six different countries to be present at the same time in the small house at Clifton Corner in New London. Curators are used to exclamations of delight from those who make the pilgrimage to the author's birthplace. "This brings back so many memories!" say many older people of the New Waterloo No. 2 stove. With its peekaboo oven where the stovepipe joins the stove, its upper tier to hold iron pots at a simmer and heavy sad and tailor's irons, and its lower tier for cast-iron cauldron and kettle, the Waterloo stove should be easily recognized by anyone who has read *Anne of Green Gables*.

The kitchen is furnished with crocks, wooden bowls, china, hooked mats and other authentic items that would have been found in every Island household during the era. It is easy to imagine how daily life may have unfolded in this house over 135 years ago. The thick, pine plank floors

bear the curves and hollows from years of wear, both from its original inhabitants as well as from a myriad of reverent visitors.

The west-facing, storey-and-a-half-high frame house where L.M. Montgomery was born was built by her paternal grandfather in the 1850s. Hugh John Montgomery and his bride, Clara Woolner Macneill, lived in the house after their marriage on March 4, 1874. Baby Maud was born on the last day of November that same year. Hugh John owned a general store called Clifton House, which was adjacent to the house at Clifton Corner. The house was home to Maud Montgomery for only a short while; her mother contracted tuberculosis while Maud was a baby and died when Maud was less than two years old. Maud was raised by her maternal grandparents eleven kilometres from her birthplace, but through the years she frequently would pass by the old home en route to her Campbell cousins' Silver Bush farm or her Grandfather

Opposite: *Montgomery's birthplace in New London*
Top: *Kitchen at Montgomery's birthplace*

Donald Montgomery's home, both located in Park Corner. "Oh, I remember making butter with this!" another visitor might exclaim upon seeing the wooden butter churn and dasher. In the small kitchen wing or ell of the house, where there are doors opposite each other — one faces the road to the west, the other faces east — so that in the summer, when the stove would give off tremendous heat during meal preparation, a welcome breeze would cool off the kitchen. In the winter, the fierce winds from the north and east still blow snow inside under the back door, where it drifts onto a hand-hooked mat of faded swans swimming in a pond.

The largest room of the house, the dining and sitting room, is adjacent to the kitchen. A large display case holding Montgomery's Island scrapbooks commands the centre of the room. These scrapbooks contain an astounding sampling of the author's rich personal life, her active social life and her extraordinary sense of colour and design. There are clippings of articles from newspapers, pressed flowers, collages of magazine pictures, patches of fur from her favourite cats, invitations the author received to events, photographs, and many other items all carefully arranged so that each scrapbook page is a visual treat and testament to the author's eye for colour and composition.

From the east window in the downstairs "parlour bedroom" — now a small sitting room — and from the north window in the parlour, the Cavendish sand spit and New London harbour can be seen. The six-over-six

Top: *L.M. Montgomery's parents: Clara Woolner Macneill (left); Hugh John Montgomery (right)*
Above: *Montgomery's Island Scrapbooks*

or 12-paned windows provide framed views of the rolling hillside which curves down to New London bay and beyond it, the Gulf of St. Lawrence. The lighthouse across from the Cavendish sand spit can also be seen from the house. Those who closely explore the surrounding area will discover a cemetery between this lighthouse and another, the Cape Tryon light, where some of the victims of the *Yankee Gale* are buried. The *Yankee Gale*, also known as the *American Storm*, struck the north shore of P.E.I. in October 1851; Montgomery writes about it in the first volume of her published journals.

The narrow parlour bedroom (approximately two by three metres) would have once been used as a place for children to nap during the day or, in times of sickness, where a convalescent could be attended to easily by the housewife.

In the parlour is a Franklin stove with an offset mantle on which a marble clock keeps time. The horsehair loveseat and matching chair set the formal tone of the parlour, as does a shadow box with an elaborate flower made of human hair, a landscape oil painting by the famous Island painter, Robert Harris (1849-1919), and a pump organ made by M. Bell & Co. of Guelph, Ontario. This room also houses a tall glass case in which the author's wedding dress is stored — an elegant, soft, off-white silk dress and lace veil made especially for Maud for her July 5, 1911, wedding to Reverend Ewan Macdonald. Every detail of the dress speaks volumes of Montgomery's lifelong love of fine clothing and jewels. The soles of her soft leather wedding shoes are stamped with the number three, although by the sizes we use today the author's foot was likely a size five. Visitors marvel at how petite the wedding dress is and, more specifically, how tiny the waist is — a mere 56 centimetres, according to the curator.

The ceilings of the birthplace are relatively low — less than a metre and a half high on the first floor and less than a metre and a quarter on the second. The overall dimensions of the house give it a cosy feeling, as opposed to a cramped one; it is often referred to as a cottage. Inside the front door is a hall. From here, a door to the left leads into the parlour and a door to the right leads to the dining or sitting room. To the far right are two steep steps and a landing. A left turn at the landing and eight more steep, shallow steps upward take you to a hall and a

Horsehair sofa

Parlour bedroom

Montgomery's wedding dress and shoes

south-facing window, which overlooks the intersection of the New London Road (Route 20) and the road to Kensington (Route 6). Directly in front of the stairs is a small bedroom that is known as the little girl's room, with a spool bed and matching wash-stand and one south-facing window. The wide, pine floorboards recall a bygone era of Prince Edward Island, when tall, white pines grew profusely and were cut down not only to build houses and furniture, but also for the thriving shipbuilding industry; Montgomery was born during the Island's golden age of sail. On the spool bed in the little girl's bedroom is a signature quilt made in 1916 by the New London Women's Institute, which raised money for the First World War effort by charging ten cents per signature. The quilt is made from bleached flour sacks, and neatly embroidered in pink thread are the names of dozens of community residents.

The bedroom in which Clara Macneill Montgomery gave birth to Maud on November 30, 1874, is long and narrow (approximately five metres by three metres) and has one north-facing window. The pine bed has an unusual array of spokes and carved pieces, topped at both head and foot with a carving of what could be a stylized thistle. A feather tick on boards and handmade quilts would have kept Clara and Hugh John warm in the unheated upstairs bedroom. A wooden crib at the foot of the bed would have held baby Maud. A chamber pot sits by the bed and an urn is by the wash-stand, where a matching china chamber set with a bowl and a water pitcher stand ready for morning ablutions.

A log-cabin afghan started by eight-year-old Sue M. Muncey is displayed in the guest bedroom located at the upstairs northwest corner. Sue Muncey was born in November of 1874 — the same month and year as the author. When she was over ninety years old, Sue Muncey, then Mrs. J.B. Leigh Lowther of Carleton, Lot 28, brought her small quilt with its miniature log-cabin pattern to the birthplace and donated it to the Lucy Maud Montgomery Foundation Trust, which administers the site. Mrs.

Lowther died on March 22, 1974, but her handiwork speaks volumes about her skill and her life; each of the thousands of tiny logs in the quilt is made from a garment from her own or her family's wardrobe. L.M. Montgomery, herself a skilled quiltmaker and craftswoman, would have appreciated the gift immensely.

The house where Maud Montgomery was born belonged to various people after Hugh John Montgomery sold it following his wife's death. In 1964, K.C. Irving, a New Brunswick entrepreneur, donated the house to the Province of Prince Edward Island in honour of the 1864 Charlottetown Conference centennial celebrations.

"Wonderful to see such a piece of history," writes a visitor in the birthplace guest book. "Enchanting. Thank you."

Room where Montgomery was born

Above: *Lake of Shining Waters, Park Corner*   **Opposite:** *The Campbells' Park Corner home, Silver Bush*

SILVER BUSH

No matter how you approach Silver Bush at Park Corner, your breath will catch at its beauty. If you arrive from the west, you will pass the gulf shoreline, known as Cousins' Shore, and the hill field where Maud Montgomery liked to sit and write. (Cousins' Shore is embossed on the 1992 Canadian twenty-five-cent piece.) If you arrive from the east, you will have travelled past Grandfather "Big Donald" Montgomery's house, perched on the gulf side of the road overlooking both sea and farmlands. Whether you arrive from the west or east you will notice a pond by the farm gate — that pond is the real Lake of Shining Waters immortalized by Montgomery's fictional Anne. A document stating the authenticity of Campbell's Pond as the real Shining Waters is signed by the author and displayed in the house. Perhaps it seems silly for anyone to document what is real about Montgomery's sources of inspiration and what is fictional about her creations, but, above all, such efforts are a tribute to the power and scope of the author's imagination. The following words are written in faded brown ink on a yellowed sheet of writing paper in

Montgomery's own hand:

To Whom It May Concern:
This is to certify that the pond at Park Corner commonly known as Campbell's Pond is the body of water I had in mind when I described the Lake of Shining Waters in Anne of Green Gables. L.M. Montgomery Macdonald October 27, 1936

Montgomery's paternal Uncle John Campbell had Silver Bush built in 1872; three years later, he married Montgomery's Aunt Annie Macneill of Cavendish. In this way, the children of Uncle John and Aunt Annie were doubly related to the author. It is with these Campbell cousins that young Maud had "so many jolly rackets" at Silver Bush. She wrote, "This is the greatest house in the world for fun." Montgomery called Silver Bush "a spacious old house," and spacious it was, with large halls and rooms, three-metre-tall ceilings, a roomy pantry and enormous windows. The formal entrance to the house faces the shore road to the northeast. A transom window sits above the wide, panelled, pine front door, which is flanked by tall sidelights.

Montgomery wanted a home of her own built from the plan of Silver Bush, and she immortalized the house in her Pat books (*Pat of Silver Bush* and *Mistress Pat*). From the stone cellar to the steeply pitched garret, the house is described in loving detail in these novels. In a letter to her penpal G.B. MacMillan dated October 25, 1933, Montgomery wrote of her newly published novel, *Pat of Silver Bush*, "I really put more of myself into *Pat* than into any other of my heroines."

What may be most remarkable about Silver Bush, the home of Montgomery's Aunt Annie and Uncle John Campbell and her Campbell cousins, is that the author's relatives still live on the 72-hectare homestead where the first Campbells settled in 1776 after arriving on Prince Edward Island from Scotland. Although the kitchen has become the entrance to the Anne of Green Gables museum and bookstore, a "fainting" couch and a replica of the original woodstove still welcome visitors to the very room where many jolly meals were cooked and served. Doors facing one another to the north and east in the kitchen ell at Silver Bush would have been opened wide to the porches in summertime, when the cookstove would make daily meal preparation a sweaty chore. A porch running the length of the west end of the kitchen would have served as a multipurpose room for donning or shedding barn clothes and boots, for storing wood and for keeping food cool or frozen in winter.

Readers of Montgomery's novels *The Story Girl* and *The Golden Road* will immediately recognize the large blue chest in the Campbell kitchen. In the books, narrator Sara Stanley recounts the sad tale of Rachel Ward, whose

Bookcase that was in Montgomery's childhood home at Cavendish and organ at Silver Bush, Park Corner, that was played at her wedding.

: *Mantelpiece in parlour where Maud Montgomery
married Ewan Macdonald
Montgomery in one of her wedding outfits*

trousseau remained locked in the blue chest after she was jilted. The contents of the real blue chest and the story behind the story can be found upstairs in Maud's bedroom. *The Story Girl* was published in 1911 and dedicated to Montgomery's cousin and closest friend, Frederica Campbell, one of the Park Corner Campbell cousins with whom Maud spent many happy days during her youth. It is fitting that the top of the blue chest is now covered with reprints of the twenty novels, numerous short stories and poignant poetry of L.M. Montgomery.

As in many farmhouses, a narrow back staircase leads to a bedroom over the kitchen, where a hired man or woman would have stayed. Montgomery readers of the Pat books will say that the bedroom over the kitchen at Silver Bush is the room belonging to Judy Plum, the fictional servant.

THE PARLOUR

If you compare the photographs Montgomery took of the parlour at Silver Bush with present-day photographs, you will see very little has changed. In fact, it wasn't until 1964 that the house was wired for electricity. Like much of rural Prince Edward Island, Park Corner was not "electrified" until the mid-1960s. The parlour bookcase with its glass doors, the pump organ and the rocking chair are the

very same ones the author knew and loved. Montgomery readers who remember Katie Maurice, Anne's imaginary friend who appeared to her in the bookcase, will look for her reflection in the old glass of the bookcase that once graced the Macneill home in Cavendish.

It is here at Silver Bush that Montgomery was married to the Reverend Ewan Macdonald at noon on July 5, 1911. The same mantle clock with its gold filigree centre still marks the hours with its faithful chime. Sharp eyes can make out the tiny printing around the perimeter of the clock's face: "Manufactured by the Graham Company, Bristol, Connecticut." Keen eyes can also see that the tassled mantle bunting or lambrequin, which is now very faded, is the same material that adorned the mantle in the author's time. The cast-iron grillwork that covers the arched parlour fireplace has at its centre a *tromp-l'oeil* garden gate, which beckons the imagination through its many-arched portal into the fire.

In her journal, Montgomery pasted photographs of herself modelling the eleven wedding outfits she had custom made in Toronto and Montreal. Accompanying the photos are swatches of the material from which each dress or suit was made. "These are the snaps the girls took of some of my dresses," she wrote on Tuesday, May 23, 1911. "The girls" referred to her Campbell cousins, Frederica and Stella. The author's elegant yet simple wedding dress is displayed at the birthplace in New London, but photographs of Maud in the clothes she had made for her honeymoon trip to Scotland were taken on the lawn outside the Campbell home. Visitors can stand by the mantle where Maud and Ewan's vows were exchanged, and sometimes even hear Maureen Campbell play "The Voice That Breathed O'er

Above: *Senator Donald Montgomery's house and farm (1880)*

Eden" on the W. Bell & Company organ on which Ella Campbell pumped out the hymn at the wedding. The pedal carpet is threadbare, but the handpainted panels with floral designs are vivid, and the ten organ stops, from bass coupler through dulcet, celeste and melodra, are all in working order.

On the bookcase desk in the parlour is a list of the twenty-four guests at Montgomery's wedding, with a newspaper description of the event:

> *The bride wore orange blossoms and a pearl and amethyst necklace, the gift of the groom, and carried a bouquet of white roses, lilies of the valley, and maidenhair fern. Many beautiful gifts were received among which was a silver tea service presented to Mrs. Macdonald by the Cavendish Presbyterian Church in which she had been a worker for many years. In the afternoon, Mr. and Mrs. Macdonald left for Montreal whence they will sail on the White Star liner Megantic for a three months' tour in England and Scotland. The bride travelled in a suit of steel gray serge with chiffon blouse and hat to match of steel [gray] braid trimmed with satin rosebuds.*

The parlour windows, two metres tall and over one metre wide, face east and north, provide views of the sloping yard, the spruce, maple and birch groves surrounding the tea room, the hiproofed barn, the Lake of Shining Waters and the rolling shore fields that hide the view of the Gulf of St. Lawrence from the first floor of the house. Through the east window can be seen Senator Donald Montgomery's house, perched on the hill overlooking the gulf.

In the large front hall is a wide staircase. Twelve steps up carry the visitor to a landing where a thick, iron screw sticks out. As a child, Montgomery used the screw to mark her height: "When I used to visit at Park Corner in the dawn of memory that screw was just on a level with my nose! Now, it comes to my knees. I used to measure myself by it every time I went over." The old, dark mirror on the wall over the screw casts a reflection, which adding mystery and subtracting years from the viewer; the interpretive card beside the mirror says it came from Grandfather Macneill's home in Cavendish "and was often used by Lucy Maud when hurrying off to school in the mornings." Five more steps bring the visitor to the large, bright, second-floor hall, where the ceilings are two and a half metres tall. Through the huge double windows is an exquisite view of the farmland sloping down to the

Montgomery's bedroom at Silver Bush

Hooked mat at Silver Bush

pond and road and then rising in gentle dunes, marshes and fields to the Gulf of St. Lawrence. It's a vista of deep blues and multiple shades of green in summer, and the white and blue shadows of a frozen landscape in winter.

Behind one of the five doorways in the upstairs hall is a set of stairs leading to a large garret composed of two rooms. The smaller room is wallpapered and was once a hired-man's room; it has a south-facing window looking onto the farm fields. The larger room contains many Campbell family possessions that have been stored and saved over the past two centuries, including the mattress tick belonging to the captain of the *Marco Polo*, a Norwegian sailing vessel that was swept ashore during a windstorm on July 25, 1883 (Montgomery first wrote about this ship in the winter of 1890 when she was fifteen years old). If you look up from the captain's tick on the garret floor through the twelve-paned window you can see the Gulf of St. Lawrence, which has as many moods as there are days in a year. A wooden ladder in the Silver Bush garret slants up to an attic, and a hatch door in the east side of the garret leads to another space over the dormer.

"MY OWN LITTLE BEDROOM"
There are six bedrooms in the Campbell home, including a downstairs guest room and a hired man's room. Mont-

gomery's childhood room is on the left at the top of the stairs; she referred to it as "my own little bedroom." It contains furniture over which she would have lovingly trailed her fingers on arrival and departure. Hooked mats lie on the floor in Maud's room, as well as in other rooms in the house. One is a traditional maple leaf and log design, with its autumn palette of oranges, reds, browns and greens still bright; another is a vine-bordered floral arrangement in vibrant colours. Through the north-facing window visitors can see the birch and spruce stand behind the new tea-room and a corner of the Lake of Shining Waters. The faux-oak finish of the three-quarters-size pine bed and matching washstand are unchanged since the author's time. A display case houses the contents of the famous blue chest, which is in the kitchen, and interpretive cards detail the real-life background of Montgomery's fictional story of the chest:

> *Eliza Montgomery came to P.E.I. from Chaleur Bay in 1847. She fell in love and planned to marry. The minister and wedding guests were here, but the groom-to-be never came. The next morning Eliza buried her wedding cake in the yard here, and packed everything in the blue chest with strict orders that it was never to be opened.*

Thirty to forty years went by. Finally, the writer visited Eliza in Toronto, and she told her to open the blue chest. They did, only to find a lot of her linen ruined, as she had so much homemade soap it had sweat the lye.

The wedding gifts were distributed among relatives of Eliza Montgomery.

The display case holds several pieces of the jilted woman's linen with the name and date "Eliza Montgomery, 1849" clearly written on them, along with gilt-edged eggcups, two lamps and a copy of a photograph of Eliza that the author pasted into her journal.

Along with all of the joyous artifacts and photographs at Silver Bush is perhaps the most excruciatingly sad document in the house, a letter that Montgomery wrote to her nephew, James Campbell, whose wife and daughter still live in the house, and whose son, George Keir, inherited the property. The entire letter is framed in Montgomery's bedroom at Silver Bush. The following excerpt clearly shows what an enormous toll the First World War had taken on Montgomery, who, as the minister's wife, had to inform families in her husband's parish that their sons had been killed in battle. Maud also worried that her own son, Stuart, would have to go to war.

```
Oct. 8, 1941
Dear Jim,
    ...I am very ill and will never see
Park Corner again.
    Don't let them stampede you into going
to war. You are more needed at home. Park
Corner would go forever if you went ... You
must not go to war. Tell them you are the
only son at home and your mother would not
live to see you come back. I can hardly
write - my nerves are so terrible. Stuart is
intern in hospital but I suppose they will
take him too. I think my mind is going.

Aunt Maud
    Rest from worry is what I need and I
cannot get that anywhere. I am done.
```

Crazy quilt made by Montgomery

STELLA CAMPBELL'S BEDROOM

As Montgomery wrote in *The Alpine Path*, her 1917 autobiography, "The Park Corner jaunts were always delightful ... Uncle John Campbell's house was a big white one, smothered in orchards. Here, in other days, there was a trio of merry cousins to rush out and drag me in with greeting and laughter."

The bedroom belonging to one of Maud's "merry cousins," Stella Campbell, is now furnished as a reading room, with autographed copies of first editions of her books that the author sent home to Silver Bush. A photograph that Montgomery herself took of Cousin Stella in her Park Corner bedroom are displayed, as is some handiwork: embroidered cotton and linen, hooked mats and dresses belonging to Stella and other members of the Campbell family.

CRAZY QUILT

Perhaps one of the most thrilling artifacts at Silver Bush is a crazy quilt, stitched and embroidered by the author and now housed in a display case in the second-floor hall. Each small piece of material was carefully cut, arranged and sewn into squares, and each square was embroidered with a multitude of fancy stitches depicting flowers, birds, names and other designs that artistically overlay the patches of bright and beautiful velvet, satin, taffeta and corduroy. A crazy quilt was the benchmark of a woman's ability with needle and thread; Montgomery's crazy quilt is an astounding accomplishment.

WAGON RIDES AND LAUGHTER

In a tea-room and craft shop built adjacent to Silver Bush, in an architectural style similar to nineteenth-century Island buildings, food is prepared according to old family recipes, and quilts and other traditional handicrafts are sold. Visitors can travel by horse and wagon to view the Silver Bush property and to follow the track from the farm to the dunes across the road and down along the gulf shore. Not much has changed here since the author enjoyed one of Aunt Annie's picnic lunches with her laughing Campbell cousins.

"There has been so much laughter at Silver Bush," Montgomery wrote in *Mistress Pat*, "that the very walls seemed soaked in it."

Top Left: *Photograph taken by Montgomery of Stella Campbell in her room at Silver Bush (1911)*
Top Right: *Wagon ride at Silver Bush*

An apple tree from Montgomery's time still blooms at the Macneill homestead

RURAL HERITAGE

For thousands of years before Europeans found their way to North America, the Mi'kmaq people lived here and called the land Minegoo, which means "the island," or Abegweit, which means "cradled on the waves."

L.M. Montgomery used the latter name when she referred to Prince Edward Island, and in an essay she wrote, published in 1939 in *The Spirit of Canada,* her nostalgia and love for her Abegweit is clear:

Peace! You never know what peace is until you walk on the shores or in the fields or along the winding red roads of Abegweit on a summer twilight when the dew is falling and the old, old stars are peeping out and the sea keeps its nightly tryst with the little land it loves. You will find your soul then — you realize that youth is not a vanished thing but something that dwells forever in the heart. And you look around on the dimming landscape of haunted hill and long sand-white beach and murmuring ocean, on homestead lights and old fields tilled by dead and gone generations who loved them — and even if you are not Abegweit-born, you will say, "Why, I have come home!"

When the Mi'kmaq people lived on Abegweit, it was a place of plenty where clams, oysters and mussels could be gathered easily from the shores. Strawberries, raspberries, blueberries, cranberries and rosehips could be picked in season, and fish, waterfowl, deer, seals and beaver abounded. When Jacques Cartier first landed here in 1534, he described the place in his diary as "the fairest land 'tis possible to see." The French first tried to establish a colony on Abegweit in 1604, and by 1700 there were a few hundred Acadians and Mi'kmaq living on Ile St. Jean, as the Island was then called. When most of North America became British territory in 1763, the Island was renamed St. John's Island, and new settlers, mostly Scottish, English and Irish, began to arrive. In 1799 the name was changed to Prince Edward Island, and by 1805 the population of the Island grew to 7,000 people. By 1881 there were 109,000 inhabitants.

MONTGOMERY'S SCOTTISH ANCESTRY

L.M. Montgomery's ancestors were among the first Scottish settlers to arrive on Prince Edward Island, before the end of the eighteenth century. The homestead now known as the site of L.M. Montgomery's Cavendish home belonged to John Macneill's great-grandparents, who were Maud's grandparents, Alexander and Lucy Macneill. The land was inherited from Alexander's father, William Macneill, who himself had inherited it from his father, John Macneill. This original John Macneill was a co-founder of Cavendish in the 1790s, and his son William, Maud's great-grandfather, was a speaker of the Prince Edward Island House of Assembly from 1814 to 1834, and was known as "Old Speaker Macneill." On her father's side, the author was connected to the Scottish Montgomery clan, and her paternal grandfather, Senator Donald Montgomery, was also a well-known figure in Island political life and a senator in the government of the Dominion of Canada. It was into this privileged and cultivated background that Maud Montgomery was born, just a decade after the 1864 conference that eventually led to the confederation of Canada.

Center: *Senator Donald Montgomery*

SELF-SUFFICIENCY

Montgomery was keenly aware and proud of her connections with the early settlement of the Island, and she wrote about her Scottish heritage in her journals and non-fiction writing as well as in her novels. The Cavendish of the latter part of the nineteenth century was a community still deeply rooted in the Scottish immigrant experience. Farming and fishing enabled the residents of Cavendish to be self-sufficient; nearly everyone at that time had what is known as a mixed farm, on which a little of everything was grown or raised, including a few pigs for pork; milking cows for butter, milk and cheese; beef cattle; ducks, chickens and geese for eggs and meat; grain for feed and flour; vegetables for the table and stock food; sheep for wool; and flax for clothing. Many fishers who worked out of New London or North Rustico harbours also ran small mixed farms, which allowed them to remain self-sufficient.

In times of misfortune, such as sickness or fire, communities were also left to their own devices. Neighbours would rush to help one another if a fire broke out, and, if necessary, a new house or barn would be built to replace one that had been damaged or lost. There were building and sewing bees or frolics in less dire times as well, when quilts were stitched, rugs hooked, barns raised and wells dug; these events were part of the social glue that held the community together.

Life during Montgomery's childhood was much more tuned to the seasons than it is today. In the spring, crops and gardens were planted as soon as the danger of frost had passed; it was generally deemed safe to plant frost-sensitive vegetables after the tenth of June. The Island's growing season is short, so every hour of fair weather was precious in the spring and everyone worked together to get the crops planted quickly. By late June and early July, the first hayfield would be ready for cutting. After it dried in the sun, the hay was pitched onto a wagon fitted with high sides and then taken to the barn, where it was pulled into the hay-loft with a huge hay-fork attached to a pulley and rope, with one end of the rope pulled by a horse. Children were expected to help with hoeing and cultivating crops and hand-picking potato bugs from row after row after row of potato plants. Sheep shearing was an annual

The Webbs harvesting potatoes and stooking grain

event; after the sheep were shorn the fleece was processed into yarn for weaving and knitting. Summers meant somewhat lighter work, although there were berries and fruits to gather and preserve, each in its respective season — from strawberries in late June to raspberries in July, blueberries in August, apples in September and cranberries from the seaside bogs after the first frost. Throughout the season, each garden vegetable would be dried, pickled or preserved for the long winter. In the autumn, before the invention of engine-driven harvesting machines,

oats, barley and wheat were cut by hand. Handfuls of cut grain were tied into bundles; twelve bundles made one "stook." Farmers stood stooks upright in the field to dry; dried stooks were then pitched onto horse-drawn wagons and hauled to the barn, where horses on a treadmill drove a threshing machine that separated the grain from the chaff. The straw was pitched into a loft for use as winter bedding for the livestock. As late as the 1960s, rural schools closed for a couple of weeks in the autumn so children could help with the harvest; there are many

Myrtle Webb on the farm at Green Gables

photographs of fields filled with young and old people, each with a handwoven basket into which potatoes were gathered. The baskets then were carried to a field cart and emptied. When the cart was full, it was pulled to the farmyard where the potatoes would be transferred — all by hand — to the root cellar, where they would keep for the entire winter. Turnips and carrots were similarly gathered and stored. Those who didn't work in the fields during harvest time would work in the kitchen to prepare hearty meals for the crew. And then there were the daily chores: splitting wood for the stoves, feeding and milking cows and separating the cream, feeding the poultry, gathering eggs and wiping down sweaty horses at the end of the day before feeding and watering them. In the winter, farmers went to their woodlots to cut trees for lumber, firewood, fence posts and longers or rails. Horses could move around fallen trees, which would then be hitched to them and hauled to an open field for cutting into lengths.

Horses were an important part of Island life in the eighteenth, nineteenth and early twentieth centuries. Even today, many families speak fondly of their former farm horses. At Orwell Corner Historic Village, east of Char-

lottetown, a draught-horse ploughing competition is held annually in autumn, and people from across the Maritime provinces bring their teams of percherons, Clydesdales and Belgian workhorses to plough a patch of field; a prize is awarded to the team and driver whose rows are most even. Toward the end of the nineteenth century, a Clydesdale or percheron could cost nearly a year's income, but a horse was invaluable; nearly all farm machinery — threshers, ploughs, hay-forks — was horse-powered.

Sustainable agriculture is a concept we in the twenty-first century are only beginning to value, but it was a way of life when L.M. Montgomery was growing up in rural Prince Edward Island. Fields were fertilized from the compost heap located outside the barns, heaps that would have received enough time to mature and heat up so that *e. coli* and other bacteria would be killed. Rich, dark, thick mussel mud was dug from tidal rivers and used on fields to build up soil. Everything was recycled and nothing was wasted.

During the late nineteenth century, the main mode of transportation would have been horse and wagon or sleigh. The railway, which was begun in 1871, zigzagged across the Island from Alberton to Souris, with stations every few miles. From Cavendish, residents would have had to travel by horse to the nearest railway station, likely either Hunter River or Kensington. Generally, however, people did not travel great distances on the Island, since everything necessary to sustain life was close at hand. Every community had its own school, church (Cavendish had two churches) and blacksmith, and what could not be fixed or mended or healed close to home would have to wait until there was time or money to travel to such larger centres as Kensington, Summerside or Charlottetown. We laugh now at the scene in the musical based on Montgomery's *Anne of Green Gables*, which has been performed every summer since 1965 on the main stage of the Confederation Centre of the Arts in Charlottetown. "Where is Matthew going?" sing the residents of Avonlea, the fictional version of Cavendish. "He should be out bugging his potatoes!" The curious community members

Top: *Cows, sheep and horses were essential to farming in the late nineteenth and early twentieth centuries*
Bottom Left: *Team of horses on an Island farm* **Bottom Right:** *Keith Webb (background) and Marion Webb*

cannot figure out why Matthew would be dressed up in Sunday clothes on a weekday and driving his mare away from the farm. The audience knows, of course, that he is going to Bright River (Montgomery's fictional equivalent of Hunter River) to fetch an orphan boy to help him on the farm. We laugh at this scene, but it is very close to the reality of Cavendish life during Maud's childhood. The community was only about five kilometres long and two kilometres wide. Everyone knew everyone else. If you did not do the laundry on a sunny Monday morning, the neighbours would be at your door with soup and baked goods, assuming that someone in the house must be gravely ill.

At Green Gables, interpretive displays and artifacts in the barn explain much about the lifestyle during the time Maud Montgomery lived in Cavendish. Activities conducted with nineteenth-century implements using the old techniques allow visitors to participate in some of the everyday chores that young Maud would have done. Chopping wood, washing clothes, making butter, hooking rugs, harnessing a horse for a wagon or sleigh ride — all of these traditional activities open windows of understanding about the physical and mental aspects of those bygone days.

Above and opposite: *Studio portraits of the young L.M. Montgomery*

LUCY MAUD MONTGOMERY
(1874-1942)

Stories behind stories: this is Montgomery's gift to us. We can read the author's own autobiography, *The Alpine Path*, first published in *Everywoman's World* magazine when she was forty-two years old, world-famous, six years married and the mother of two young children. We also can read the journal she kept from 1889 to the end of her life in 1942. And if we also read the letters she wrote to George Boyd MacMillan during their thirty-nine-year friendship, and to Ephraim Weber, with whom her correspondence lasted a similar length, from 1902 to 1941, we will be better equipped to examine the many facets of the author, which she presented in various forms to various audiences: to herself, to her close friends and to her current and future readers.

MONTGOMERY SLEUTHS

There have been a number of brilliant Montgomery sleuths over the past quarter century who have chronicled and interpreted the author's life and works. These include Dr. Elizabeth Waterston and Dr. Mary Rubio, editors of Montgomery's journals; Dr. Elizabeth Epperly, literary scholar and passionate Montgomery reader; Dr. Francis W.P. Bolger, whose 1974 *The Years Before "Anne"* presents the author's life from the viewpoint of an Island-born historian. It was Elizabeth Waterston who wrote about Montgomery long before the author was considered worthy of the literary establishment or canon. Waterston's essay, "Lucy Maud Montgomery, 1874-1942," published in 1966 in *The Clear Spirit: Twenty Canadian Women and Their Times*, is considered the landmark essay on Montgomery. Waterston begins her study by stating that fairy-tale language "seems to be the first way to tell the story of Lucy Maud Montgomery."

The facts of Montgomery's early childhood can be presented in ways that make a listener either groan with pity or exclaim in envy. However the raw material is presented, we can be sure that Montgomery herself viewed it in a multitude of ways and mined its depths for her own imaginative fiction.

She was born in 1874, the year after Prince Edward Island joined Confederation, and was orphaned, or nearly so, twenty-one months later. She was a young child during an era of Island history now regarded as "golden," when the small province was self-sufficient and prosperous. The Northumberland Strait and the Gulf of St. Lawrence were filled with fish — cod, hake, mackerel, redfish, bluefin tuna and dozens of other species, including lobster and other types of shellfish. The woods were old-growth or virgin forests, with tall white pines, beeches, red oaks and other hardwoods and softwoods that were used for the thriving Island shipbuilding industry. The farm fields with their thick hedgerows were fertile, and marsh hay was free for the cutting.

Montgomery's father, Hugh John, owned and operated Clifton House, a store at Clifton Corner adjacent to the little house where he and Clara Woolner Macneill lived after their marriage on March 4, 1874. Maud was born in the upstairs bedroom of the house on a hill overlooking New London Bay on November 30, 1874. Her mother contracted tuberculosis while Maud was a baby, and both mother and child went to Cavendish to be cared for by Clara's mother, Lucy Macneill. Three months shy of her daughter's second birthday, Maud's mother died. Maud's earliest memory was of seeing her mother lying in her coffin in the Macneill parlour. She remembered putting her hand on her mother's cheek and wondering why she lay so still. Alexander and Lucy Macneill raised Maud; she would eventually tend to them in their old age.

CAVENDISH CHILDHOOD

The nearest railway station to Cavendish was a 19-kilometre horse-and-wagon ride away, and the nearest town twice that distance. But the community had nearly everything it needed: a blacksmith, a general store, two churches, a community hall, a school, orchards, farms, a post office and a wharf nearby. Cavendish had been settled in the late 1700s by three families who had emigrated from Scotland to the New World: the Macneills, the Simpsons and the Clarks. The clannishness of the families was part of their Scottish background, and it manifested during Maud's childhood as an expectation that she would honour her clan in deportment and behaviour and that she be

Top: *Montgomery's photograph of her bedroom at Cavendish.*
Above: *Montgomery, Kate Macneill and friend on the shore at Cavendish (c. 1890)*

The approach to the crossroads at Cavendish. Green Gables farm is on the right (1920)

pious, proper and proud of her kin. At the time, there was a consideration that some of the well-established and relatively wealthy founding families, including the Macneills, thought they were cut from better cloth than certain other members of the community. There is evidence of a certain social and intellectual snobbery in Montgomery, which might very well be traced to her early years in Cavendish.

Throughout her life, Montgomery harkened back to what she came to value as an ideal childhood. The freedom she had in her youth, roaming the seashore and following meandering paths through the woods and farm fields, would seem extraordinary to children today. Maud and her Macneill cousins and school chums would lose themselves in adventures, absent from adult scrutiny after school and during the long summer days. Maud would often visit her Grandfather Montgomery, whom she adored, in Park Corner, in a house she described as "full of cupboards and nooks, and little, unexpected flights of stairs." And she would also frequently visit her Uncle John and Aunt Annie Campbell and her cousins at Silver Bush, where she had her own little room. Each brook and corner of field, each hedgerow, every pond and shore cave had its own mystery and delight, and to the imaginative, adventuresome Maud, nature was her finest teacher.

Maud had a lifelong affection for houses and for housekeeping; she was an excellent cook, needleworker, gardener and decorator. The photographs she took of her favourite rooms — the kitchens at the Macneill and Campbell homes and, later, her own kitchens at Leaskdale and Norval; the parlours; her bedrooms; the exteriors of her favourite houses; and the curves in lanes and nooks in fields — are all tributes to her fondness for and appreciation of domestic life.

PASSION FOR CATS
No portrait of Montgomery would be complete without mentioning her love of cats. Montgomery would one day call the death of a kitten when she was nine her "baptism of sorrow," and describes herself as having gone nearly mad with grief over the poisoned grey kitten. Cats were

One of the author's favourite cats.

Montgomery's soulmates. Bobs, Topsy, Pussywillow, Catkin, Daffy, Pat, Brownie, Lucky and Paddy — all of the cats in her life, as well as those in her fiction, are now immortalized. There was no self-consciousness in Montgomery's ardent, often-articulated adoration of cats. Of the several thousand photographs she took over her lifetime, a great number of them are portraits of her beloved feline friends.

FIERCE AMBITION
In 1893, after she received her first tangible reward for her writing — two subscriptions to an American magazine in payment for the publication of her poem "Only a Violet" — Montgomery wrote in her journal, "Oh, I wonder if I shall ever be able to do anything worth while in the way of writing. It is my dearest ambition." Montgomery expressed a crucial goal in her life with those words: the desire to write something worthwhile and lasting. She could always differentiate when she was doing "hack" writing as opposed to when she was writing from the heart or writing something worthy of her own praise. The title Montgomery chose for the 1917 story of her career came from *The Fringed Gentian*, a verse that she had clipped from a magazine and saved as "the key-note of my every aim and ambition": "How I may reach that far-off goal/Of true and honoured fame,/And write upon its shining scroll/A woman's humble name."

SCHOLARSHIP AND TEACHING

In 1890, Montgomery travelled across Canada to Saskatchewan to spend a year with her father, stepmother and half-brother Carl, and to attend high school in Prince Albert. A year away from Cavendish was plenty, and she returned in the autumn of 1891, too late to rejoin her classmates at school, so she spent a year at home, finishing school the following year with high marks in the provincial examinations that every student at the time was required to take. In 1893-94, Montgomery boarded in Charlottetown, where she accelerated a two-year teacher's course at Prince of Wales College into one year, after which she took a teaching position at Bideford, a rural community at the western end of Prince Edward Island. She boarded at the Bideford Parsonage, which has been restored to represent the era when Montgomery lived there. All during her Prince of Wales and Bideford teaching days, Montgomery continued to write and to publish her stories and poems in magazines.

Following a year at Dalhousie College in Halifax, Nova Scotia, Montgomery took another teaching position, this time in Belmont, Prince Edward Island, where she stayed during 1896-97. It was here that she became engaged to Edwin Simpson, a Baptist minister. In the autumn of 1897, she took yet another teaching position, in Lower Bedeque, where she fell in love with Herman Leard, a young farmer about whom she writes passionately in her journal. She broke her engagement with Edwin Simpson while she was in Bedeque, and then also rejected Herman Leard, considering him to be beneath her both intellectually and socially.

Grandfather Macneill died while Montgomery was teaching in Bedeque, and at the end of the year she returned to Cavendish to help Grandmother Macneill with the farm and post office. Montgomery remained there from 1898 until her grandmother's death in March 1911. Four months later, Montgomery married Ewan Macdonald, the Presbyterian minister to whom she had been secretly engaged for five years. Except for the seven months in 1901-02 when she worked as copy editor for the *Daily Echo* in Halifax, Montgomery stayed with Grandmother Macneill — a dozen years during which she was prolific, writing her first novel, *Anne of Green Gables*, in 1905, hundreds of short stories and poems and three more novels: the first Anne sequel, *Anne of Avonlea*, *Kilmeny of the Orchard* and *The Story Girl*.

During the years she spent in Cavendish looking after her grandmother, Montgomery renewed her friendship with her cousin Frederica Campbell, who became her closest friend. Frede, as she was often called, later went on to study and teach household science at Macdonald College in Montreal. Maud was active in the social life of Cavendish, including the literary society and the Cavendish Presbyterian church. When the Governor General of

Cavendish school c.1900

L.M. Montgomery (left) and pupils at Belmont school

Canada came to Prince Edward Island in 1910, he asked to meet Montgomery, as he was a fan of her work. The story of their meeting is a humorous one: Governor General Earl Grey invited Montgomery for a private stroll and conversation and chose to sit on the steps of the Macphail homestead outhouse, a decision that amused Montgomery during their discussion, as she noticed baffled guests approaching the outhouse and quickly turning away, not wanting to embarrass the esteemed visitor, who obviously was not acquainted with country ways.

HOME IN LEASKDALE

After a three-month honeymoon in England and Scotland, Maud and Ewan settled in the Presbyterian manse in Leaskdale, Ontario, and Montgomery began her new life as Mrs. Ewan Macdonald, minister's wife. Between 1912 and 1915, Montgomery had three children: Chester Cameron, born in July 7, 1912; Hugh Alexander, stillborn on August 14, 1914; and Ewan Stuart, born October 7, 1915. Hugh Alexander's small gravestone is located in a country cemetery in Zion, Ontario, midway between Uxbridge and Leaskdale. On September 8, 1914, Montgomery wrote in her journal, "our wee darling lies there in a little green corner under the elms."

During her Leaskdale years, Montgomery revised a collection of stories and published them under the title *Chronicles of Avonlea*, and wrote and published two new novels, *The Golden Road* and *Anne of the Island*. Montgomery's worldwide fame continued to grow, with translations of her works available in several countries. Her American publishers, L.C. Page & Company of Boston, demanded sequel after sequel about the red-haired orphan Anne Shirley. The first movie version of *Anne of Green Gables* was made in 1919.

From her journals, we can see what a toll the First World War took on Montgomery, who followed every battle in newspapers and on radio and who, as minister's wife, had to inform parishioners of the loss of their sons and comfort them as best she could. When her dearest friend and cousin, Frederica Campbell, died of Spanish influenza in

Mr. and Mrs. Ewan Macdonald on their honeymoon

1919, Montgomery wrote that she did not know how she would survive the loss. During this same period, Ewan suffered a nervous breakdown, and Montgomery had to carry the responsibilities of their children, their home and Ewan's parish duties on her own shoulders. She was always careful to maintain the dignity of her family, going to great lengths to cover for Ewan, sometimes even writing his sermons for him. As well, Montgomery had to endure two vicious lawsuits against her publisher, who had cheated her out of royalties, sold reprint rights illegally and published a book of her early stories against her wishes. Montgomery eventually won both lawsuits, but she spent much money and energy in the process.

The tragedies Montgomery experienced during and after the First World War find a creative and transformative outlet in *Rilla of Ingleside*, a novel that tells stories both of Canadians on the battlefields and of those who stayed behind to keep homes and farms going.

The moon burst triumphantly through an especially dark

cloud and shadow and silver chased each other in waves over the Glen. Rilla remembered one moonlit evening of childhood when she had said to her mother, "The moon just looks like a sorry, sorry face." She thought it looked like that still — an agonized, careworn face, as though it looked down on dreadful sights. What did it see on the western front? In broken Serbia? On shell-swept Gallipoli?

One of the main characters in the story, a young man named Jem, writes home from the front:
We have been under fire since the last week in February. One boy — he was a Nova Scotian — was killed right beside me yesterday. A shell burst near us and when the mess cleared away he was lying dead — not mangled at all — he just looked a little startled. It was the first time I'd been close to anything like that and it was a nasty sensation, but one soon gets used to horrors here. We're in an absolutely different world. The only things that are the same are the stars — and they are never in their right places, somehow.

Tell mother not to worry — I'm all right — fit as a fiddle — and glad I came. There's something across from us here that has got to be wiped out of the world, that's all — an emanation of evil that would otherwise poison life for ever. It's got to be done, dad, however long it takes, and whatever it costs, and you tell the Glen people this for me. They don't realize yet what it is has broken loose — I didn't when I first joined up. I thought it was fun. Well, it isn't! But I'm in the right place all right — make no mistake about that.

In 1922, while she was at Leaskdale, Montgomery wrote *Emily of New Moon*, the first of the Emily series. It was published the next year, the same year Montgomery was named the first Canadian woman to become a member of the British Royal Society of Arts. Perhaps it was this honour that prompted Montgomery to recopy the diaries she had kept from 1889, sensing that she would receive

Above: *Portrait of L.M. Montgomery when she received an OBE (1935), and Mr. and Mrs. Ewan Macdonald on a boat trip on Georgian Bay, Ontario*

62

fame after her death and that her diaries would interest her millions of readers. A foreshadowing is found in the final line of *Emily of New Moon*, the most autobiographical of all of Montgomery's works: "I am going to write a diary, that it may be published when I die."

LIFE AT NORVAL

In 1926, Ewan Macdonald accepted a new parish in the town of Norval, Ontario, and the family moved into the brick manse by the church. Montgomery continued to publish novel after novel, including *The Blue Castle* in 1926, the only one of her novels not set in Prince Edward Island. Instead, it is set in Bala in the Muskoka Lake region of Ontario, where the Macdonalds had spent a summer vacation several years earlier. In 1928, both Chester and Stuart left for boarding school, and Montgomery was alone again with Ewan, whose illness, called "religious melancholia" in those days, was severe; his bad days outnumbered his good ones. Montgomery went on a speaking tour across the Canadian West in 1930, and the following year published *A Tangled Web*, a novel for adults. Chester entered the University of Toronto to study law in 1931, and in 1933 Stuart went to medical school. Stuart completed his medical degree and practised for many years in Toronto. In 1934, Ewan's illness was serious enough that he had to be committed to a mental hospital for four months.

JOURNEY'S END

When Ewan retired in 1935, he and Maud decided to move to Toronto, where Maud found a house she liked overlooking a ravine. She fittingly named the house "Journey's End." She was made an officer in the Order of the British Empire in 1935; the photograph of her taken for the occasion clearly shows how proud she was to have received the honour. That same year, Montgomery was elected Fellow of the Royal Society of Arts and Letters. While she lived at Journey's End, Montgomery continued her involvement with the Canadian Author's Association and the Women's Press Club. She published more novels:

the Pat series, *Anne of Windy Poplars*, *Jane of Lantern Hill* and *Anne of Ingleside*, and movie rights were sold for a talking version of *Anne of Green Gables*.

In 1937, Montgomery's health declined and she suffered a nervous breakdown. At this point, Ewan was too deep in his own mental illness ever to recover. In 1939, Montgomery visited Prince Edward Island for the last time. She was unable to face the reality of the outbreak of the Second World War, and she became profoundly depressed. She died broken-spirited on April 24, 1942. Her body lay in state in the Green Gables house, and the funeral was held in Cavendish Church. She was buried in Cavendish cemetery not far from the graves of her mother, grandmother and grandfather. A year later, Ewan died; his body was buried beside Maud's on the hill gravesite she had chosen because from it she could see the blue Gulf of St. Lawrence to the north, and in every other direction lay the fields and woodlands she had cherished while she was alive.

Old Cavendish church and graveyard as they looked during Montgomery's childhood. Montgomery and her husband are buried here.

"THE CUP OF SUCCESS"

In her afterword to the New Canadian Library edition of *Emily of New Moon*, Canadian writer Alice Munro praises Montgomery's ability to allude to the story behind the story. "There's life spreading out behind the story — the book's life — and we see it out of the corner of the eye. The milk pans in the dairy-house ...The corners of the kitchen ... at New Moon."

At the age of fifteen, seated between Sir John A. Macdonald, the Prime Minister of Canada, and his wife, Lady Macdonald, on their special train that had stopped at the Kensington Railway station to pick up the young Maud and her paternal grandfather, Senator Donald Montgomery, Maud was not so star-struck as to lose her writerly passion for observation. "I sat demurely and scrutinized them both out of the tail of my eye," she wrote in her diary on Monday, August 11, 1890, at the end of that exciting first day of her cross-Canada journey. She was setting out for western Canada, where she would spend a year living with her father, and her Grandfather Montgomery had telegraphed his political crony Sir John A., who was visiting the Island, to make a special stop at Kensington to take them on his train.

A WRITER'S EYE

Throughout Montgomery's journals and works of fiction are many examples of how she scrutinized people out of the "tail of her eye," and just as many examples of how she permitted us, as readers, to see into the corners of places, see life spreading out beyond the story in the foreground. L.M. Montgomery was an intense observer of life. When her journals were published, the first volume of which was available in 1985, we were able to find much primary evidence of her ability to see and to write what she saw, and then to create imaginary scenarios and characters from this raw material. Montgomery's journals, ten legal-sized volumes in total, are the finest imaginable source that show us how her life as a writer unfolded.

Montgomery said that she kept a diary from the time she was "a tot of nine," but that she burned her early efforts and began a new approach to diary-keeping on Saturday, September 21, 1889, when she was nearing her fifteenth birthday. On that day she vowed to keep her diary locked up. She obviously considered herself a mature person as she set out to keep her new diary, much too mature for the childish entries of the burned diary, which she said was dull and "told what kind of weather it was." "Life is beginning to get interesting for me," she states. She goes on to talk about an old geranium she has named Bonny, boldly asserting she believes the plant has a soul.

SOULS OF PLANTS

When Anne first arrives at Green Gables, she is stunned by the beauty of the place, a state which Marilla clearly does not understand. When Anne waves her hand to signal the expansive view from her window and says to Marilla, "Oh, isn't it wonderful?" Marilla replies, "It's a big tree, and it blooms great, but the fruit don't amount to much never — small and wormy." And so Anne begins to educate her new guardian:

"Oh, I don't mean just the tree; of course it's lovely — yes, it's radiantly lovely — it blooms as if it meant it — but I meant everything, the garden and the orchard and the brook and the woods, the whole big dear world. Don't you feel as if you just loved the world on a morning like this?"

When Marilla and Matthew decide that she can stay at Green Gables, Anne goes on to name every tree, brook, hollow and nook around her new home and to invent stories and dramas about each one. Like her fictional Anne, Montgomery named geraniums, trees, cats, ponds and lanes — she was always particularizing the world around her; yet, in an instant, she could widen her point of view from a specific bird or bush to understand and articulate the universal processes of life. Small and large natural phenomena — day into night, night into day, seasonal changes, birth and death — evoked awe in Montgomery and stimulated her to find the words to express first and foremost to herself, and only secondarily to her readers, the joy, sorrow, delight or mystery each phenomenon created. Similarly with people and social situations, Montgomery constantly sought the best phrase, sentence, paragraph, poem or story to reflect an emotion or event in all its subtlety and complexity.

TEENAGED CRITIC

Imagine the accomplishment and self-knowledge reflected in fifteen-year-old Maud's comments to herself in her diary on February 19, 1890, about a schoolmate's essay for a competition held by the Montreal *Witness*. Montgomery's essay was about the wreck of the *Marco Polo*, and her chums wrote about the Yankee Gale that struck the north shore of the Island in October of 1851. "I am not afraid of Asher but Nate will run me close. He is a good writer. I read his essay today and I am afraid it is better than mine. But I thought it a trifle too florid in style."

Whether or not a twenty-first-century critic would categorize Nate's essay as "a trifle too florid," Maud was correct in at least part her assessment; Nate's essay ranked higher than her own, although she came next, and she notes in her diary that her effort came third for Queen's County. The Montreal *Witness* published her account of the shipwreck in February 1891, and the story was copied by the Charlottetown *Daily Patriot* on March 11, 1891. The first work of Montgomery's ever published was not this essay, however, but a poem she wrote in November of 1890 about the legend of Cape Leforce, which she secretly sent to the newspaper back home from Saskatchewan, where she was living with her father and his second family. When mail from the Island reached her in Prince Albert early in December 1890, Montgomery discovered that her poem had been published, and she wrote in her diary that it was "the proudest day of my life." She said in her autobiography, *The Alpine Path,* that the publication of her verses "was the first sweet bubble on the cup of success, and, of course, it intoxicated me! ...The moment we see our first darling brain-child arrayed in black type is never to be forgotten. It has in it some of the wonderful awe and delight that comes to a mother when she looks for the first time on the face of her first-born." When she wrote these words, Montgomery had already given birth to her three children.

The 104-line poem The *Wreck of the Marco Polo* marked the beginning of Montgomery's life as a published writer. From those early days to the end of her life, Montgomery witnessed hundreds of her "brain-children" set to type. In all, she published twenty novels, five hundred short stories, five hundred poems and many essays. In addition to this, Montgomery wrote a million and a half words in the ten volumes of her journals, and she was an inveterate letter writer — there are collections of her letters to Penzie Macneill, George Boyd MacMillan, Ephraim Weber and many other correspondents.

Montgomery was born into a family that valued education, books and reading. The small library at the Macneill home in Cavendish included classics of English and Scottish literature, and as assistant to her Grandmother Macneill, the Cavendish postmistress who operated the post office from the kitchen wing of the Macneill house, Maud saw and read all of the newspapers and mostly American monthly and periodical magazines that arrived at the post office. Maud's privileged position in the post office also later assured her that no one but herself saw manuscripts leave the Island nor saw some of them, notably the manuscript for *Anne of Green Gables*, returned, rejected, time after time.

While Montgomery was in Halifax in the fall of 1895 taking an English literature course at Dalhousie College, she received notice of the acceptance of one of her short stories by a Philadelphia juvenile magazine called *Golden Days*. How did twenty-one-year-old Maud spend the five dollars enclosed with the acceptance? It was the first money she had ever earned from her writing, and with it she bought five volumes of poetry by Milton, Byron, Tennyson, Longfellow and Whittier, thereby marking the occasion of having "arrived," as she put it.

During an April snowstorm in 1903, Montgomery wrote in her journal that her "only guard against absolute misanthropy" was re-reading books from the Macneill library, including Nathaniel Hawthorne's *The House of the Seven Gables*, Washington Irving's *Alhambra*, George Eliot's *Adam Bede* and Edward FitzGerald's translation of *The Rubaiyat of Omar Khayyam,* which she described as "a string of pearls threaded on the blood-red cord of an oriental fancy." She reflects on the last in a journal passage about the elusiveness of happiness and goes on to lament, "I'm

Portrait of Montgomery (1894)

tired of existence. Life has been a sorry business for me these past five years. I don't think anybody suspects this. To those around me, even my most intimate friends, I am known as a 'very jolly girl,' seemingly always light-hearted 'good company' and 'always in good spirits.' It makes me laugh rather bitterly to hear people say this. If they could only see below the mask! I am thankful they cannot. I don't want to be pitied ..." She goes on to say what a comfort her journal is to her, and the next entry after the gloomy one of April 12, 1903, is made on the last day of June of 1903, when the weather is beautiful and she has spent a happy month with her good friend Nora Lefurgey.

Throughout her journals and letters, Montgomery writes about what she is reading, and her taste was eclectic and wide-ranging — poetry, literary fiction, gardening,

L.M. Montgomery (1930) on one of her last visits to Prince Edward Island

beth Waterston, have indexed the numerous book titles discussed or referred to by the author in her journals.

PORTRAIT OF THE ARTIST AS A YOUNG GIRL

More than any other of her works of fiction, *Emily of New Moon* and its sequels, *Emily Climbs* and *Emily's Quest*, offer an insider's look at a writer and the art of writing. Montgomery herself said that the first Emily book was the best book she had ever written: "I have had more intense pleasure in writing it than any of the others — not even excepting Green Gables. I have lived it, and I hated to pen the last line." From the opening chapter of *Emily of New Moon* to its last words, "I am going to write a diary, that it may be published when I die," the novel gives us a portrait of a developing writer. Emily's "flash" of inspiration is accompanied by an intense need to find the right words to describe whatever produced the flash. In chapter one of the first Emily book, for instance, "there was a sudden rift in the curdled clouds westward, and a lovely, pale, pinky-green lake of sky with a new moon in it." After clasping her hands in joy and awe, Emily's sole desire is to go home and write a description of the scene; Montgomery writes, "it would hurt her with its beauty until she wrote it down." We can extrapolate from Montgomery's insights about writing in the Emily series, and from parallel experiences in the author's journal, that her own quest was to ease her soul's vibrations with both the beauty and the pain of life by writing.

Montgomery is an adept storyteller. Although the plots of many of her novels and short stories might be conventional, her ability to weave a compelling story is always apparent. Montgomery was born into a family of storytellers and into an era of storytelling. She gives special credit to her Aunt Mary Lawson, really her great-aunt, who was one of the children of William ("Old Speaker Macneill") and Eliza Townsend Macneill, the author's great-grandfather and great-grandmother. "No story of my 'career' would be complete without a tribute to her," Montgomery wrote in 1917, "for she was one of the formative influences of my childhood." Montgomery

current psychological and scientific thought, psychic phenomena, spiritualism and politics were just a few of the subjects that interested her. She was extraordinarily intelligent and versatile, and she possessed a perspicacious mind. In her works of fiction, many of her most admirable characters are also readers or writers. How many young readers around the world have been first introduced to and then drawn to read Tennyson's poetry after reading chapter 28, "An Unfortunate Lily Maid," in *Anne of Green Gables*? Here, the melodramatic Anne, "devoured by secret regret, that she had not been born in Camelot," plays the lily maid Elaine. Draped in Marilla's black shawl, she drifts in a leaky, flat-bottomed dory, borrowed from Diana Barry's father, on the pond below Orchard Slope. The editors of Montgomery's journals, Mary Rubio and Eliza-

L.M. Montgomery (right) and Myrtle Webb in Lover's Lane

admired her Aunt Mary Lawson's high intelligence, re-markable memory and ability to be a "brilliant conversa-tionalist." She wrote, "I cannot, in any words at my com-mand, pay the debt I owe to Aunt Mary Lawson." Aunt Mary Lawson's eye for detail, ear for vernacular and long, sharp memory provided Montgomery with the equiva-lent of a doctorate in storytelling. It is easy to imagine the teenaged Maud and the seventy-odd-year-old Mary Lawson side by side on walks in the woods or performing a household chore, one the avid apprentice, the other the master teller who has finally found a suitable heir.

Even as a mother of two small children and with the increasingly onerous duties of minister's wife as her hus-band's mental health steadily declined, Montgomery maintained her daily writing regime. She understood from having crafted stories, poems and diary entries throughout her life that daily practice kept her faculties sharp. Her inner drive to write is evident in her journals; her need to meet publishers' and readers' demands for more stories provided an external impetus. The money she earned from her writing was another incentive; it was Montgomery's income, not her husband's meagre minister's salary, that kept the household together financially. Montgomery in-vested some of her income in a number of companies and was affected, but not devastated, by the October 1929 stockmarket crash. Through the years, she loaned money to friends, many of whom never repaid her, and she paid for the private school and college education of her sons.

The profoundly satisfying artistic aspects of her writ-ing would have sustained Montgomery through many trying years when her husband was less and less able to face his parish, not to mention his inability to cope with his family as his mental condition worsened. By times, Montgomery's writing may have provided her the island of sanity otherwise missing from her daily existence.

In 1908, Montgomery penned the "Island Hymn," which became known as Prince Edward Island's "patri-otic hymn"; the manuscript copy is located at the Green Gables tourist centre. Although she composed the words three years before she left her Island home to live in On-tario for the rest of her life, the lyrics of the third verse have an eerie foreshadowing of the author's deep nostal-gia for her childhood home: "Prince Edward Isle, to thee/ Our hearts shall faithful be/Where'er we dwell;/Forever may we stand/As brothers, hand in hand,/And sing God save the land/We love so well."

CANADIAN HEROES

In the spring of 1999, the Dominion Institute and the Council for Canadian Unity conducted a survey to find out whom Canadians considered to be their heroes. Na-tionally, in English and French, more than 28,000 people responded to the survey, nominating both living and dead Canadians. Among the top twenty Canadian heroes was Lucy Maud Montgomery, who ranked among the likes of Sir John A. Macdonald, Tecumseh, Laura Secord, Alexan-der Graham Bell, Louis Riel and Nellie McClung. And on the eve of the year 2000, in a national CBC Radio poll that asked the public who they thought were best Canadian writers of the twentieth century, Montgomery ranked first.

Montgomery's novels are translated and published in dozens of countries. Her international recognition and popularity were once stumbling blocks that kept her from being embraced in the literary canon, but now she takes her rightful place in the academy, as well as in the hearts of millions of readers.

PRESERVING THE MEMORY

A key part of preserving the memory of L.M. Montgomery is the challenge of maintaining the integrity of the land that inspired the author throughout her life. In 1937, the Canadian government set aside a forty-kilometre stretch of the north shore, from the western tip of the Cavendish sand spit in New London Bay to the beginning of the sand spit that lies across Tracadie Bay, a coastal landscape known as a maritime plain. Encompassed by Prince Edward Island's national park are many of the places known and loved by Montgomery: freshwater ponds, salt marshes, sand dunes, forests and cultural sites such as the Green Gables house and farmlands. Within the park's boundaries, there is a certain amount of restriction as to how the land may be altered, and as residents become more educated about the impact of tourism on a finite piece of land, more restrictions on development are put in place so that the landscape that the author immortalized in her writing does not disappear altogether under pavement.

In 1994, a group of concerned north-shore residents began the L.M. Montgomery Land Trust, a registered non-profit organization that aims to preserve the area. "The blending of carefully cultivated farmland with the unfettered beauty of the coastline gives Prince Edward Island a distinct beauty that is our greatest heritage resource," states the Land Trust manifesto. The Trust preserves heritage land through active conservation and responsible land management. Property owners may give land to the Land Trust by gift or will, or the Land Trust can purchase prop-

erty from a land owner. As well, property owners may sell or donate their land, but they retain the right to live on it for the rest of the lives. With guidance from the Land Trust, property owners may place restrictions on future development of their land or sell the Land Trust development rights to their land. In this way, the Land Trust hopes to preserve the pastoral landscapes that Montgomery experienced, and from which she drew lifelong sustenance.

The original tract of land on which David Macneill Senior built his farm spanned 54 hectares. The land was passed on to his son, David Macneill Junior, in 1887, and David and his unmarried sister Margaret Macneill lived together in the house. When Margaret lost her eyesight, Myrtle Macneill, David Jr. and Margaret's niece came to live with them. In 1905, Myrtle married Ernest Webb. The couple lived in the Macneill house and ran the farm. As Montgomery's fame grew after the 1908 publication of *Anne of Green Gables*, so too grew the fame of the fictional house that was based on the Macneill–Webb home. The Webbs renovated the house so that they could accommodate summer visitors. Montgomery herself often stayed with them, as her own home nearby had been left vacant and was eventually torn down, and as she was friends with Myrtle and Ernest's children, Marion, Lorraine, Keith, Anita and Pauline. Anita went to Ontario to work for Maud and her husband for a while, and later, Marion, who married Murray Laird of Norval, Ontario, also worked for them. Keith Webb also moved to Norval. Late in her life, Montgomery recopied her cookbook, which contained all the Macneill, Montgomery, Campbell and Webb family recipes, as well as recipes from the many friends Montgomery had made on the Island and in Leaskdale and Norval. Montgomery gave the original cookbook, a leather-bound ledger, to Anita Webb, who was by then a professional cook. The original has survived, and in 1996, Marion Webb Laird's daughter and granddaughter published *Aunt Maud's Recipe Book*, a collection of recipes from Montgomery's cookbook.

The decision to make the Cavendish area a national park was largely undertaken because of the popularity of the Green Gables house, which by the 1930s was the destination of thousands of devoted Montgomery readers. The house was bought by the government in 1936 and leased back to the Webbs, who continued to live in the kitchen wing. Ernest Webb was hired by Parks Canada to conduct tours of the house, something he had already been doing unofficially for many years. The Prince Edward Island National Park opened in 1937. In 1946, the government bought a new house for the Webbs, and officially opened Green Gables to the public four years later. Early visitors to Green Gables sipped tea in the kitchen; it was not until 1967 that a gift shop and tea-room separate from the house were opened. Early in the morning of May 23, 1997, a fire broke out at Green Gables. Firefighters arrived on the scene quickly and were able to limit the damage. Matthew's room and the sewing room above it were the worst hit, and many antiques were damaged by smoke and water. By noon offers of help were received from as far away as Japan, and many people donated antiques to replace the ones that had been lost. All was repaired and Green Gables reopened on Canada Day, only thirty-eight days after the fire broke out.

The L.M. Montgomery Heritage Society was organized in 1993 and consists of representatives of sites, organizations and other groups that have a strong connection to Montgomery's life and works. The Society is dedicated to the preservation of Montgomery's literary and cultural legacy, and it is committed to ensuring the authenticity, integrity and historical accuracy of all initiatives pertaining to the author. The Society also coordinates such events as annual celebrations of the author's birthday and summer festivals in the Cavendish area, which are co-sponsored by the L.M. Montgomery Land Trust. Every August the Heritage Society hosts an interfaith service in memory of the author at the Cavendish United Church, to which Montgomery donated the church organ when she left the area in 1911.

The L.M. Montgomery Institute at the University of Prince Edward Island was the founded in 1993, the inspiration of Montgomery scholar, Dr. Elizabeth R. Epperly. The goal was to develop research projects that further the local, national, and international understanding of the life and work of L.M. Montgomery. The Institute has hosted eight international conferences; the ninth, entitled "L.M. Montgomery and the Matter of Nature," is to be held in June 2010. Collections of essays based on the L.M. Montgomery Institute's symposia have been published by the University of Toronto Press. In 2000, the Institute produced a multi-media CD entitled *The Bend in the Road: the Life and Works of L.M. Montgomery*, which won seven local, national, and international awards, including three at the 2000 Baddeck International New Media Festival. The Institute works closely with the Montgomery family, with the L.M. Montgomery Heritage Society, with the heirs of L.M. Montgomery, with the Land Trust, and with the provincial government's Anne of Green Gables Licensing Authority.

In the Montgomery world, there is co-operation and collaboration on many levels in order to honour the name of one of Canada's most loved authors — the world famous L.M. Montgomery.

Acknowledgments

This book has come into being with the generous help of the following people: the Macdonald family and Heirs of L.M. Montgomery Inc.; Brenda Dunn, Parks Canada, Halifax; Doug Heaney, Parks Canada, Green Gables, Cavendish; Barbara MacDonald, Parks Canada, Charlottetown; John and Jennie Macneill, Site of Montgomery's Cavendish Home: Dr. Francis W. Bolger and Vivian Fyfe, Lucy Maud Montgomery Foundation Trust; George Campbell, Park Corner; University of Guelph, MacLaughlin Library, Special Collections; Prince Edward Island Public Records Office; Dr. Mary Rubio and Dr. Elizabeth Waterston; Dr. Elizabeth Epperly; and the L.M. Montgomery Institute at the University of Prince Edward Island.

Anne of Green Gables, Green Gables House and other indicia of "Anne" are trademarks and Canadian official marks of the Anne of Green Gables Licensing Authority Inc., which is jointly owned by the heirs of L.M. Montgomery and the Province of Prince Edward Island, and are used under licence by Formac Publishing Co. Ltd.

L.M. Montgomery is a trademark of the Heirs of L.M. Montgomery Inc.

Bibliography

Bolger, Francis W.P. *The Years Before "Anne": The Early Career of Lucy Maud Montgomery.* Halifax: Nimbus Publishing Limited, 1991.

Bolger, Francis W.P. and Epperly, Elizabeth R., eds. *My Dear Mr. M: Letters to G.B. MacMillan from L.M. Montgomery.* Toronto: Oxford University Press, 1992.

Crawford, Elaine and Crawford, Kelly. *Aunt Maud's Recipe Book.* Norval: Moulin Publishing Limited, 1996.

Kessler, Deirdre. "L.M. Montgomery and the Creation of Prince Edward Island" in *L.M. Montgomery and Canadian Culture.* Edited by Epperly and Gammel. Toronto: University of Toronto Press, 1999.

McCabe, Kevin, compiler and Alexandra Heilbron, ed. *The Lucy Maud Montgomery Album.* Toronto: Fitzhenry & Whiteside, 1999.

Montgomery, L.M. *The Alpine Path: The Story of my Career.* Markham: Fitzhenry & Whiteside Limited, 1997. Originally published in 1917.

———. *Anne of Green Gables.* Toronto: McGraw-Hill Ryerson Limited, 1968.

———. *Emily of New Moon* by L.M. Montgomery. Toronto: New Canadian Library Edition, McClelland & Stewart Inc., 1989.

———. *Rilla of Ingleside.* Toronto: Seal Books, McClelland-Bantam Inc., 1973.

Munro, Alice. "Afterword" to *Emily of New Moon* by L.M. Montgomery. Toronto: New Canadian Library Edition, McClelland & Stewart Inc., 1989.

Quayle Innis, Mary. *The Clear Spirit: Twenty Canadian Women and their Times.* Toronto: University of Toronto Press, c. 1966.

The Bend in the Road: An Invitation to the World and Works of L.M. Montgomery, CD-ROM. Charlottetown: L.M. Montgomery Institute, 2000.

Rubio, Mary and Waterston, Elizabeth, eds. *The Selected Journals of L.M. Montgomery, Volumes I-IV.* Toronto: Oxford University Press, 1985, 1987, 1992, 1998..

References

p.7 Selected Journals II:38,Selected Journals II:39-40; p. 10 *Anne of Green Gables,* 34; p. 13 Selected Journals II:39, *Alpine Path,* 29; p. 24 *Anne of Green Gables,* 213-14; p. 29 *Alpine Path* 47; p. 30 Selected Journals II:38 ; p. 33 *Lucy Maud Montgomery Album,* 30; p. 34 *Lucy Maud Montgomery Album,* 28; p. 35 Selected Journals I:331; p. 44 *My Dear Mr. M,* 168; p. 46 *Alpine Path,*43; p. 48 *Alpine Path,*43; p. 57 *The Clear Spirit*; p. 61 Selected Journals II:154; p. 62 *Rilla of Ingleside,* 144, 97; p. 65 *Emily of New Moon,* 360-1; p. 66 *Anne of Green Gables,* 34-5, Selected Journals I:17; p. 66 Selected Journals I:35; p. 66 *Alpine Path,*38, 61; p. 67 Selected Journals I:286; Selected Journals I:287; Selected Journals, III:39; p. 68 *Alpine Path,* p.15

Photo credits

Photography by Alanna Jankov with the following exceptions:
T= Top, B = Bottom, R= Right, L = Left
Kindred Spirits of PEI / John Sylvester, p. 43; L.M. Montgomery Collection Archival and Special Collections, University of Guelph Library, p. 23 (T), 33, 34 (L), 38 (TL & TR), 45 (BR), 49, 56, 57, 58 (T & M), 59, 60, 61, 62, 63, 64; Meacham's Illustrated Historical Atlas of PEI 1880; NAC RG 84 Vol. 150 PEI 1313, p. 13 (T); Parks Canada, p. 10, 53 (B), 54, 58 (B); Parks Canada (Marion Webb Collection) p. 13 (M), 53 (T), 55 (BL & R); PEI Public Archives and Records Office/ PEI Museum and Heritage Foundation Collection p. 52, 55 (T)